A2 Drama and Theatre Studies

Carolyn Carnaghan   John Davey   Alan Evans   Steve Lewis
Consultant: Ginny Spooner
Guidance on Unit 4 by Alan Perks

STUDENT BOOK

A PEARSON COMPANY

Contents

Introduction

Welcome to A2 Drama and Theatre Studies. In following this course, you will further develop the skills gained during your AS studies. Drawing on your practical experiences studying the plays in Unit 1, and developing your own performances in Unit 2, you will have the opportunity to explore the creative process of preparing and performing an original piece in Unit 3.

In Unit 4, you will draw again on your practical experience, and also your evaluations of live performances in Unit 1, to explore plays and performances in their historical context: both as a director, and also as an active audience member.

In all these areas, you will gain skills and understanding that will prove to be valuable and rewarding into the future.

What plays will you explore?

For Unit 3, you will create your own unique performance, based upon a stimulus provided by your teacher – which could be a published play. In Unit 4, you will study one of three set plays, chosen by your teacher: *Lysistrata* by Aristophanes (c. 411BC); *Doctor Faustus* by Christopher Marlowe (c. 1594); *Woyzeck* by Georg Büchner (1837). You will also study one of the three periods of theatre history represented by these plays, though not the one your set play belongs to.

How can you make Drama and Theatre Studies rewarding?

During your AS studies, you will have:

- spent your time working practically with others

- realised that there are no 'right' or 'wrong' answers

- worked as an individual in researching material and putting your knowledge and understanding down on paper.

During the A2 year, building on your learning at AS, you will:

- develop a more advanced level of performance and/or production skills

- learn to think independently, make judgements and refine your work in the light of research

- analyse the ways in which different performance and production elements are brought together to create theatre

- learn to appreciate the historical and cultural context of a live performance and the decisions a director makes in his interpretation of a play.

How are you assessed?

There are two units in this A2 course.

- In Unit 3: Exploration of Dramatic Performance, you work collaboratively to create a unique and original piece of theatre. You will be required to provide a written record of the piece's development. Your work is marked by your teacher and externally moderated.

- In Unit 4: Theatre Text in Context, there are two sections. The first section requires you to study a set play from the point of view of a theatre director. The second section requires you to see a live performance of a play and to study and research its original performance conditions. You will be assessed in a written examination lasting two-and-a-half hours.

The Assessment objectives

There are four Assessment objectives that will be used to assess your work. These are explained in the table below, along with a guide to which parts of the course each objective relates to. In the units you'll find more detailed guidance on what is required for each element of assessment.

Assessment objective		What do you have to do?
AO1 (40%)	Demonstrate the application of performance and/or production skills through the realisation of drama and theatre.	This objective is assessed in Unit 3. For performers, it refers to your vocal and movement skills in performance. For designers, it refers to the way you use materials and equipment, and how you realise your design in performance.
AO2 (20%)	Demonstrate knowledge and understanding of practical and theoretical aspects of drama and theatre using appropriate terminology.	This objective is assessed in Unit 4 through the written examination.
AO3 (30%)	Interpret plays from different periods and genres.	This objective is assessed in Unit 4 through the written examination.
AO4 (10%)	Make critical and evaluative judgements of live theatre.	This objective is assessed in Units 3 and 4 through an evaluation of your own performance and Section C of the written examination.

How to use this book

This book is designed to support you with the range of activities you will undertake in your A2 year of Drama and Theatre Studies. A Planning, Teaching and Assessment Guide is available to support the Student Book.

The Student Book builds on your learning at AS and supports the two units of the course, providing:

- clear explanations of what is required of you, what you need to do, and how you will be assessed, along with examiner tips
- Unit 3: a clear and practical guide through the creative process of developing your own piece of theatre, offering support on the decisions you will face and how best to prepare your Supporting Written Evidence documents, backed up with six detailed case studies, two of which are provided as recorded performances in the Planning Guide
- Unit 4: an introduction to the set plays and their historical periods, with guided support in exploring these practically and through research, directly aimed at preparing you for the demands of the written examination
- structured support in developing your analysis and evaluation skills, and putting your knowledge and understanding down on paper
- the Examzone sections, supported further in the Planning Guide, give clear guidance on preparing for the exams and detailed support on how to tackle them.

We hope that you will enjoy furthering your study of drama and theatre and wish you much success with the course.

Ginny Spooner, Edexcel

A2 Drama and Theatre Studies

In your A2 year, you will find it helpful to continue the good working practices that you developed during the AS year. In this section, we look at some of the practical issues that you will need to continue to bear in mind.

Working methods

In lessons, you'll be working as you often have before: recording information, notes and thoughts, or responding to worksheets, whiteboard prompts, and so on. The organisation and filing of these notes are important and you should try to do them promptly. It's a good idea to use ringbinders (with dividers), keeping a different file for each unit (and sections within units).

When researching, you'll need to record details of your sources. This includes:

- titles, authors and page references (books/journals/magazines)

- website addresses (as well as titles/authors where relevant)

- quotations that you have copied down from sources (highlighting can be a useful method).

For practical sessions, you may well need to make preparatory notes or plans and make sure that you have these with you. During the session, you may need to make brief notes to capture information or to remind yourself of points/ ideas, and you'll have to get used to making notes while being active. You may also find yourself writing down moves in your text. Near the end, or possibly just after the session, you will need an opportunity to make fuller notes so that no information is lost, or to remind yourself about what you have agreed to organise, prepare or think about for the following session. You may follow this up at home by expanding these notes or grouping them.

> **Tip**
>
> Take pencils, a sharpener and eraser to all your sessions. Pencils are preferable to pens when you're working on texts and changing ideas, moves, and so on. Ideas are provisional and experimental, and will be changed or overwritten. Highlighters are also useful for highlighting words in a text, for example using a different colour for relevant stage directions. You can use them too for marking key words in your notes.

Resources: thinking ahead

As well as your own resources, you'll be using the resources of your school or college and possibly some other resources as well. This needs a bit of thought on occasions, and a small amount of planning can save you a good deal of time.

- **Space**: for your lessons, you'll be allocated working space. If you want to use space outside your normal classes to rehearse a scene or to develop an improvisation, you will probably need to make special arrangements to book it. There may be health and safety issues involved which need to be considered.

- **Props and costumes**: these are not always easy to come by, particularly if you have specialist requirements such as period costumes or wigs. Don't underestimate the time, difficulty and expense involved in locating and accessing these. For workshop sessions, rehearsal props and costumes are usually very satisfactory for giving you the feel of the real thing – and they're much easier to obtain.

- **Lights, sound, special effects**: if you are intending to use these, you will need to plan and probably take advice, as there will be health and safety issues involved here.

The most important thing with the use of all these resources is not to make assumptions, but to plan thoughtfully.

Unit 3: Exploration of Dramatic Performance

- It is worth 40% of your A2 mark (20% of the total A-level marks).
- It is internally assessed (marked by your teachers) and externally moderated (by Edexcel).

What you have to do

You must apply the knowledge and skills developed during your AS studies to *create* a unique and original piece of theatre from a stimulus provided by your teacher. You must work in groups of no fewer than three and no more than six and perform the work in front of an identified audience. You must keep a detailed record of your research and exploration during the process, and complete an evaluation of the process and the performance of the work.

How you are assessed

- Your teacher will assess your involvement in the development and structure of your work throughout the creative process as well as the final performance in front of an identified audience.
- You need to submit written evidence of your research and exploration for the piece.
- You must also write an evaluation of both the process and the final performance of the work.
- The assessment by your teachers will be externally moderated by Edexcel.

Content	Assessment requirements	Percentage of Unit 3 marks allocated	Format
Creation of a unique and original piece of theatre	Research and exploration	25%	Written
	Development and structure	25%	Teacher monitored
	Performance	25%	Live
	Evaluation	25%	Written

How the unit builds on your AS work

For Unit 1, you will have studied several plays in terms of how they are structured and interpreted. Your practical exploration will have allowed you to understand the language of theatre, encouraging you to respond imaginatively to a range of specific stimulus material.

For Unit 2, you will have contributed to a group interpretation of a selected play for an audience, and experienced live performance as an individual or with a partner in your monologue/duologue performance. Your knowledge and understanding of how plays are constructed and interpreted for delivery to an audience will enable you to create your own unique performance in a group context within Unit 3.

One of the most influential aspects of your AS year will have been the wide range of professional performance work that you have seen. It is expected that you will be influenced by the work that you see, and you should not hesitate to incorporate appropriate ideas into your own devising.

The demands of the unit

The process of creating new work is clearly an ensemble (group) activity, and throughout the process the whole group must understand the importance of working towards the same vision for the piece. The material developed will depend upon:

• the direction and purpose decided by the group

• your experiences during the first year of the course

• the strengths and interests of individuals

• the expertise and facilities available in your centre.

Whatever the focus, the creative process depends upon six key factors:

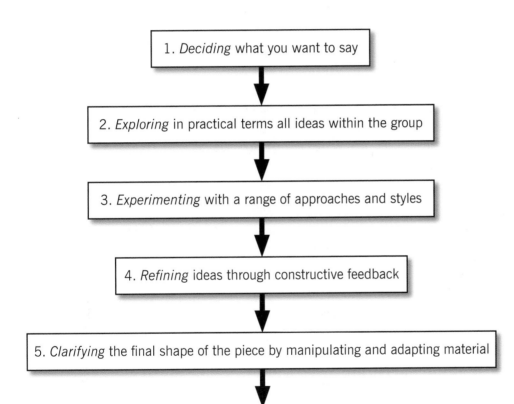

1. *Deciding* what you want to say

2. *Exploring* in practical terms all ideas within the group

3. *Experimenting* with a range of approaches and styles

4. *Refining* ideas through constructive feedback

5. *Clarifying* the final shape of the piece by manipulating and adapting material

6. *Polishing* the work to performance level

PERFORMANCE

Agree the group rules before you start

It is very important to establish from the beginning that all group members are willing to operate within a set of agreed rules. You should agree these at the start, but do not spend too long on this task.

The process demands its own set of skills, and every member of the group must understand the value of:

- being present at all rehearsals/workshops
- working in a focused and practical manner during every session
- considering feedback from the teacher and each other, and being prepared to respond accordingly
- researching and thinking about the work between sessions
- being cooperative and focused on the purpose of the work
- ensuring that all opinions are heard and explored.

It is essential that every member of the group:

- is open to creative opportunities (wherever they come from)
- tries to be innovative
- is prepared to accept constructive criticism
- is willing to reject elements that do not suit the piece
- reflects frequently and encourages group self-evaluation
- remains constructively critical at all times
- plans realistically and within resource constraints
- adheres to deadlines
- retains their focus on the stimulus and the target audience.

Activity 1 (group)

Spend 10 to 15 minutes discussing the points above, then draw up the working rules for your group that you can all agree to.

Disagreements are inevitable, and you must not allow them to upset group harmony. It is important to be honest with each other and accept that criticism is not personal, but aimed at improving the finished product.

Making decisions

For Unit 3, you must create a response to:

- stimulus material, themes, ideas or issues; or
- a published play.

The initial stimulus will be determined by your teacher, but whatever the starting point, you must decide the following:

- What is your subject, or what do you want to say?
- Who is your audience?
- Where do you want to perform?
- What theatre/practitioners or styles of performance inspire you?
- What expertise do you have?

The first question is often the hardest to answer, but often determines the next two points.

Tip

This task can use up much of your available time with limited progress.

Different audiences will react to performances according to their previous experiences and expectations of what they hope to see. For example, an audience of drama students will probably be more informed about theatrical conventions than a group of science students. Elderly audiences in retirement homes will not necessarily appreciate the same material as a group of year five school pupils.

It is very important that you decide upon your target audience at the earliest possible stage in the development of your work. Sometimes the style of the performance will be determined by the stimulus and this in turn will dictate the audience that you aim at; however, you might decide from the outset that you want to perform for your local primary school and this decision will guide your initial experimentation and ideas.

Once you have agreed on the potential audience for your work, it is useful to find out what they know about either theatre or the subject of the work to help you create the right content. You must also make sure at the earliest opportunity that you can ensure access to your chosen audience; it would not be good to create a piece for your local primary school and then find that they cannot find the time or space for you to perform. Similarly the choice of audience will often impact upon the space that you perform in. If you choose to create work to be delivered in the local shopping mall, then you will need to be aware of the many issues with this style of performance as well as obtaining the essential permissions from the local authority.

Deciding your audience early will enable you to make sure that all the associated issues can be considered and resolved.

The work or approaches of specific practitioners that you decide to explore further during the development of the work will depend upon your experiences as a group in your own centre. The productions you have been to see and the methods of theatre directors and writers will influence your work. If your experience of theatre has been within the naturalistic style and you have applied the ideas of Stanislavski, you may decide that you want to select this style of play or devised piece to work on. Conversely, you might wish to explore the work of a very contrasting theatre practitioner such as Bertolt Brecht.

You will be influenced by the plays you have seen and, if you have been in the audience of productions by Frantic Assembly or Théâtre de Complicite, then you may wish to use some of their techniques and staging devices.

In the case studies, it is clear that the groups have been inspired by plays they have been to and workshops they have taken part in. For example, in Case study 1, the group used ideas from a **commedia** workshop to create archetypes and, in Case study 3, the students attempted to achieve the same style of performance as they had used in a previous play. In Case study 4, the ideas of Constantin Stanislavski about creating believable characters on stage were very important and, in Case study 5, the group selected Artaud and DV8 as the practitioners whose ideas would be most appropriate for the group and the piece.

Key term

Commedia dell'arte

Key terms

brainstorming
convention
cross-cutting

Tip

When you know your starting point, it is important that you don't talk about what you could do, but get up and experiment!

Tip

If your starting point is an existing play, then you will need to read it carefully, together with any commentaries on it. When you are familiar with the play, you will need to discuss within your group the *aspects* you wish to focus on, the particular meanings you want to convey, or the style of performance you want to use to convey your ideas.

Activity 3 (individual)

Select a play that you have some knowledge of, and decide what ideas within it you could explore with your group. Be ready to explain your suggestions to the rest of the group.

The activity below is to familiarise you with the process of **brainstorming**.

Activity 2 (group)

Choose three of the starting points listed below. Spending only ten minutes on each, write down any ideas you have. Don't look for 'clever' ideas – just put down whatever comes into your head.

The big blue	Teenage drinking	Phobia
Junk or treasure?	In too deep!	Who cares?
A question of trust	The recycling issue	Homeless youth
The fame game	More front than Brighton	Living in a goldfish bowl
I think I know you	A question of trust	Chemical escape

Many groups spend valuable time looking for the 'completely original' idea; *it does not exist.* Everything has been investigated through the medium of theatre. What you need to do is find an interesting and engaging approach to whatever subject matter you choose.

Whatever theme, idea or issue you start with, the exploration stage is critical. Even before the research stage, you need to brainstorm the stimulus individually, write initial thoughts on a large sheet of paper and then explore practically as many of them as you can within the time limits. Don't decide the direction or format until you have tried all the ideas – even though many will lead to nothing. Be open and flexible and see what develops; often quite simple thoughts can generate other ideas and avenues for investigation.

It is often helpful to use familiar exercises and games, or workshop activities to energise the group and ensure that you do not spend time discussing theoretical possibilities at the expense of practical experimentation.

It is useful to capture these explorative activities on video for reviewing later to help with selecting and refining your choice.

Some theatrical **conventions** (strategies) you could use include:

Dialogue	Overlapping dialogue	Hot-seating
Direct address	Silence	Role reversal
Tableaux	Exaggeration	Marking the moment
Freeze-frame	Puppetry	Reportage
Flashback/forward	Song	Vox pop
Thought-tracking	Mirror work	Photograph
Narration	Masks	Image theatre
Choral speech	Still image	Forum theatre
Ensemble movement	Re-enactment	**Cross-cutting**
Ritual	Mime	Choral work
Dance		

Developing the idea

Unless you have a member of the group who wants to offer directing as their individual skill, all members of the group must take responsibility for offering ideas and developing the work through discussion, experimentation and critical feedback. If you have a member of the group acting as **director**, they will become the eyes and ears of the group and, using your ideas, will mould them to achieve the intended outcome for the whole group.

Once you decide to pursue an idea, you need to continue experimenting, usually through **improvisation**, to further the development and inspire more ideas.

'Improvisation' is a generic name for any unscripted piece of drama. It is frequently used to investigate and explore ideas that might develop into polished performance. Many professional companies, particularly those involved in creating small-scale touring work, use the technique to initiate or develop ideas for their productions. Many improvised ideas will not lead to usable results. This should not be a concern, because you are using the procedure to 'try out' initial ideas. Case study 1 (page 25) is a good example of a group searching for ideas and methods in the early stages of their work.

Remember to keep a detailed record of your exploratory work for your Supporting Written Evidence document; a log or diary that records the practical process is ideal for this purpose. Your Supporting Written Evidence document must show your research and early exploration of the subject matter, performance style, play text, creative methods or experimentation with techniques. This is discussed in more detail on page 61.

Your involvement in developing and structuring the work will be monitored and assessed by your teacher(s) and will constitute 25 per cent of the available marks for the unit.

The table below shows the criteria that your teacher will use to mark your contribution to the development and structure of the performance based on your involvement in the process. Key words and phrases have been underlined to remind you of the focus for your involvement.

> **Key terms**
>
> director
> improvisation

> **Practitioner note**
>
> Some theatre directors rely heavily on their actors to improvise around ideas before they write the final script. Joan Littlewood used this approach with her group at Stratford East Theatre in London, and Mike Leigh uses a similar method when creating his films and theatre scripts.

Assessment criteria	Level of response	Mark range
AO1 Development and structure	Students demonstrate an <u>outstanding involvement</u> in the developmental process with a creative and imaginative input that has a <u>far-reaching benefit</u> to both their own work and the work of others.	13–15
	Students demonstrate an <u>excellent involvement</u> in the developmental process with a creative and imaginative input that <u>fully benefits</u> both their own work and the work of others.	10–12
	Students demonstrate a <u>good involvement</u> in the developmental process with a creative and imaginative input that <u>benefits</u> their own work and some of the work of others.	7–9
	Students demonstrate an <u>adequate involvement</u> in the developmental process with a creative and imaginative input that <u>impacts</u> on their own work but has <u>little impact on the work of others</u>.	4–6
	Students demonstrate a <u>limited involvement</u> in the developmental process. They incline towards <u>accepting creative ideas</u> made by others with <u>little understanding or appreciation</u> of their relevance to the intended performance.	0–3

Your teacher(s) will assess your involvement *throughout* the creative process.

The aspects that they will be considering are:

Contribution to group discussion/practical exploration

Innovation and imagination	Adaptability
Exploration of techniques	Application between group sessions
Listening skills	Cooperation
Reflection	Attention to detail
Characterisation	Commitment

How long will your performance be?

For groups of three or four, your performance should last about 15 to 20 minutes, and for groups of five or six, about 30 minutes; this is not long, but a great deal of research and process work is needed. It is essential that only the best moments from your creative efforts are included, and this means that you must be selective and make difficult decisions about what to reject. Often performances are too long because group members feel that everyone should have the same amount of dialogue or exposure. It is important that every actor makes a significant contribution, but the time on stage or number of lines do not equal marks. It is the *level of skill* and *ability to engage with the audience* that are assessed during the performance.

Check it out!

Tip

Make sure they are not simply saying what they think you want to hear!

You can become too familiar with the content and shape of the piece that you create, and it is important to check its impact with as many people as possible. If your initial idea was to create a comic piece and no one finds it amusing, you might want to think again! Perform for as many people as you can who represent your target audience. Get their opinions of the work by asking specific questions; remember you know what is intended, but you need to make sure that your audience understands.

Tip

Don't be defensive – you need to know what is and isn't working.

The best people to consult are those with some expertise in theatre or the subject matter of your work. Other drama and theatre students are often a valuable source of constructive criticism. Consult your specialist teachers as they can advise you on what will work and what will not; they cannot 'direct' your work, but can guide you by asking challenging questions.

If you can, record the work frequently. Watching it between development sessions can be helpful in deciding the most effective moments. Do not use practical session time to watch the recordings; every second of the creative process is valuable.

The finished piece

The finished piece must be performed for the particular defined audience for whom it was created. The performance counts for 25 per cent of the marks for this unit and must be treated as a professional production. Make sure that the audience gets a true theatre experience.

Remember that the production has to be recorded and that all group members must be clearly identified at the start. This is best done some time before you need to warm up for your performance, but 'in costume' so that you can be easily recognised in action.

The table below shows the criteria that your teacher will use to mark your performance. Key words and phrases have been underlined to remind you of the focus for your performance.

Assessment criteria	Level of response	Mark range
AO1 Performance	Students demonstrate <u>outstanding skills</u> within the compass of their chosen role or roles within the assessed performance. Their contribution to the performance <u>comprehensively communicates their intentions</u> to the audience.	13–15
	Students demonstrate <u>excellent skills</u> within the compass of their chosen role or roles within the assessed performance. Their contribution to the performance <u>fully communicates their intentions</u> to the audience.	10–12
	Students demonstrate <u>good skills</u> within the compass of their chosen role or roles within the assessed performance. Their contribution to the performance <u>communicates a range of intentions</u> to the audience.	7–9
	Students demonstrate <u>adequate skills</u> within the compass of their chosen role or roles within the assessed performance. Their contribution to the performance <u>communicates some intentions</u> to the audience but these lack consistency.	4–6
	Students demonstrate a <u>limited range of skills</u> within the compass of their chosen role that <u>communicates</u> its worth to the audience <u>in a fragmentary and haphazard way</u>.	0–3

The finished piece must be polished and engage your target audience in the desired manner. It is important to stress that the work does not need to have any significant social message, but might simply be designed to entertain. It must, however, clearly communicate your intentions to the audience, and relate to the original stimulus. Throughout the process, you will need to consider the nature and size of the venue, the actual performance space and technical resources available (see page 21).

Your group may have students who wish to be assessed as a **designer** or director and this will affect the way in which your group operates (see pages 20–24).

Key term

designer

Two tramps from a production of *Waiting for Godot*

Some key components

When shaping the work and deciding which moments are most effective, you will need to ensure that you have considered some of the basic elements of theatre such as plot and action, roles, contrast and tension to highlight or colour the drama.

Plot and action

As in most stories, the plot, if you have one, must be clear or at least engaging throughout. Your work need not have a conventional beginning, middle and end, and you do not have to represent a continuous timeline. Whatever the structure, the events on stage must be coherent, and delivered to create a specific impact or emotion in the audience. To use conventions effectively, it is sometimes useful to focus on what effect you aim to have on the audience. All the case study groups, with the exception of group 5 (page 49), ensured that the structure was clear for their audience; group 5, working in a very Artaudian manner, was more concerned with creating the right impact through the work.

Theme and issue

Often, the ideas or issues that are what any play is really about are not the same as what actually happens (the plot). For example, *Waiting for Godot* seems to be about two tramps waiting for someone called Godot, but there are many theories about what the play is really saying about the human condition; some argue that it is about marriage, others that it is about the nature of belief.

When you work on your own piece, you must decide what you want it to convey to your audience. The style and manner of your performance will dictate whether your meaning is obvious or hidden. All the case study groups, with the exception of group 6 (see page 55), focused their work on a particular issue or viewpoint that they wanted to convey.

Focus

You need to be sure that you are directing the audience's attention to the most significant moments in your work. For example, three performers walking around the stage space conveys very little. If they are walking around the space looking for a lost contact lens, there is a clear focus. If they are searching for the code to defuse a bomb and have only 20 seconds left, there is focus *and* tension.

Normally the character speaking and/or moving will have the audience's attention, but the audience focus can be manipulated by the performers. If three characters are standing and one sitting, the latter is likely to be the focus of attention. If six members of the cast are stage right looking at one person stage left, the latter will be the focus.

You can use stage positioning, levels, dialogue and action to determine where the audience should be focused. Cross-cutting (moving the action from one group to another) is a typical method of directing the audience's attention. Several of the case studies mentioned ensuring that their focus for specific moments was clear.

Activity 4 (group)

Use the opening of any play with three or four characters.
a) In groups of three or four, discuss where you want the audience focus to be.
b) Explore practically different methods of directing the audience's attention.
c) Show the other groups your ideas in performance and discuss how effective they were.

Tension

Tension is the force that engages the performer and audience in the dramatic action. It suggests stress or argument, but should perhaps be thought of more in terms of friction or difference. Tension may be represented as: person against person; person against environment (external force, physical nature, society or 'fate') or as person against herself/himself (conflict with some element in her/his own nature, maybe physical, mental, emotional or moral).

Tension can show differences of opinion, disagreement or pressure (all of which may be comic). It may occur at an important point in a dramatic event; something disastrous, unusual or unexpected may be about to happen. Sometimes the tension may be set up quite crudely as a direct confrontation between characters, or with the audience. This provides an effective way of releasing or directing the participants' energy. At other times, tension may take the form of a dilemma, a threat, a pressure posed by an outside source or by time factors that demand some kind of response in the near future.

Tension can be used to move the action forward, create focus, pace or surprise. Silence is also a powerful foundation of dramatic tension and suspense. Some simple methods to create tension are language (and silence), stage positioning, levels and patterns of movement, thought-tracking or narration (see the list of conventions on page 10). Case study 2 (page 32) has clear examples of the use of tension.

Activity 5 (group)

a) Move around the performance space.

b) An object in the room (a hat, for example) alternately attracts and repels the whole group.

c) Decide upon a corner of the room and as a group point to it and move towards it with menace.

d) Repeat, but without pointing or any discussion.

e) Group forms a protective circle around two blindfolded performers. In the centre of the circle is a bag of jewels (any object). One is the thief, the other the security guard.

f) Group clap: the aim is to clap simultaneously without a signal. Pass the clap. Stand with right palm facing up, left palm facing down. Pass the clap round the circle.

g) In pairs, improvise various scenes (at the doctor's, shopping, meeting the boss, etc.). A piece of string joins the pair; when it is tight, play the scene with high tension, and when slack, with low tension.

Character

In performance, you will assume a character other than your own, from personal observation or from the imagination. You will need to adopt the physicality, attitudes and beliefs of the character you are playing. The character adopted might determine relationships, action, and may even affect the setting. A character may be **naturalistic**, **representational**, **stereotyped**, and within some styles, quite abstract, grotesque or surreal.

Key terms

naturalism
representational
stereotype

You may decide that you need to 'multi-role', and portray a range of characters that might cover a variety of types. Pages 12–16 of the AS Student Book discuss how you begin to develop your vocal and physical skills. For the A2 student who has had two years of practical experience, it is important that your performance skills are appropriate and effective for the selected style. The case studies on pages 25–60 show how the students ensured that their individual performances were suited to the effect they wanted to create for the target audience.

Mood

> **Key term**
>
> production

This is the atmosphere you create on stage through all aspects of performance and **production**.

Establishing and changing the mood within your work allows you to concentrate the dramatic action and affect the audience emotionally. The ending of Case study 1 (page 25) is an excellent example of the creation of a specific mood, and most of the case studies contain this element.

Activity 6 (group)

a) Select three different pieces of music.

b) Decide as a group what mood, atmosphere or feelings are suggested by each piece.

c) Develop three freeze-frames that capture the mood of each piece.

d) Move from one image to the next, using a word that sums up the mood.

e) Play a scene set in a busy office. One group member changes the music, and the rest must continue the action in the appropriate mood.

Contrast

This element is used to vary the pace of the drama, build atmosphere and a sense of occasion, and create tension. A period of energy might be followed by a period of calm and reflection, or a brightly lit atmosphere changed to one of half-light or darkness. Working in groups in tight areas might be opened up with the use of different levels or a larger space; an activity involving ritual might be destroyed by the arrival of a character or other incident. Case study 2 (page 32) has clear examples of the use of contrast.

Symbol, metaphor and ritual

These involve the use of objects, gestures or people to represent meanings beyond the literal. They are ancient aspects of drama and theatre that tap into the rhythm of life. You need to be sure that each is used in an imposing and purposeful way.

Symbol

Symbols have layers of meaning. Whereas an image has one meaning, a symbol often has many. Often the symbol is an object that signifies something much greater than its functional use.

A key, used as a symbolic object, may stand for freedom or captivity (depending on the context). A battered suitcase may symbolise the struggles or travels of a refugee. The character focuses seriously on this object, perhaps using slow and deliberate gestures when handling it. This allows the depth of its importance to be communicated to the audience. In Case study 5 (page 49), the group used the toilet pan as a symbol of the girl's bulimia.

Activity 7 (group)

a) Each member of the group brings in an object.

b) Explain to your group the significance that the object could have.

c) Use the object in an improvised scene to show its importance.

d) Repeat with each object.

Metaphor

Metaphor operates in a similar way to symbol, but on a more overarching scale. The whole context can be a metaphor and can also work with character; for example, the 'company boss' character may represent a tyrant. In that context, the company would be a metaphor for the state. The character of Arturo Ui is a clear example of this.

Ritual

As in daily and public life, ritual has a place in drama. Making a cup of tea can be a ritual repeated in times of trouble, offering comfort in its familiarity.

Ritual in drama usually involves a heightened, noble, and almost awesome or reverential way of doing things. It can be used to build atmosphere and tension and give depth to your work.

Candidates in Case study 5 (page 49) decided on a form of ritual with the placing of the toilet pan.

Activity 8 (group)

a) Pass an object around the group as if it were a symbol of authority.

b) One member of the group moves around the performance space and the rest must show that he/she is their leader.

c) In groups of three or four, create a ritual for the handover of power from one leader to another.

d) Create a chant that welcomes home a brave warrior.

e) Create a movement and sound sequence to summon the spirit of Summer.

Practitioner note

Symbols are often used by designers to suggest, sometimes subconsciously, the meanings within the drama. For example, at a production of *Arturo Ui* at the Library Theatre in Manchester, a huge pile of battered shoes at the side of the stage provided a constant reminder that the comedy on stage was a comment on the rise of Nazism and its atrocities.

Tip

Royal Hunt of the Sun by Peter Shaffer is a good example of how ritual can be effective on stage.

Language

The word choices made and the enunciation of the actors often move the plot and action along, provide exposition and define character. The delivery of dialogue is affected by the performers' choice of tempo, rhythm, volume and intonation. The language of the play can also refer to the choices made by the writer and/or performer in relation to the intensity or register of the words used. For example, a play might use language that denotes a typically British garden party, or by contrast a group of women working in a clothing factory. In the same manner, the use of accent can denote location, status or relationships to other characters.

Each playwright often creates their own specific style regarding the language they use in establishing character, location or environment. There is an interesting use of language in the reporter scene in Case study 1 (page 25), and in Case study 6 (page 55) language is used to create misunderstandings and enhance the comedy.

Visual elements and spectacle

The visual qualities determined by the group will help to create the world and atmosphere of the play for the audience. Spectacle within production can involve all of the aspects of scenery, costumes and special effects. Similarly, the performance aspects such as movement around the space, character positioning, use of levels, gestures, facial expression and use of masks or make-up can create specific theatrical effects. You will see that Case study 5 (page 49) relies heavily on movement and sound with almost no logical dialogue, but all the groups consider how their work will appear on stage.

Polishing the product

Many candidates at this level create an effective structure for the piece, but fail to polish the work sufficiently to gain maximum marks. Remember: 25 per cent of the possible marks for this unit are achieved through the quality of the performance. You must rehearse the finished work until it becomes automatic, but at the same time making sure that familiarity does not lead to complacency.

Keeping it fresh

The group in Case study 1 (page 25) used some of the suggestions below to ensure that they did not become bored with the work, and this helped them to maintain their levels of energy and input.

- Decide as a group that a particular run-through will be done as your favourite cartoon characters, with strange accents, funny walks or in a particular genre such as melodrama, opera, TV soap, horror movie, or game show.
- Similarly, to make sure that lines are totally secure, the group can sit in a circle and do a 'speed run' of dialogue; set a record and try to beat it next time.
- If the performance has defined scenes, then try 'top and tail' runs where performers deliver the first and last line of each scene.
- Movement runs allow you to confirm the patterns of stage movement throughout the piece, and these can also be linked to 'fun' conditions.
- Try performing the work without dialogue, using only freeze-frames as you might see in a comic book.

The methods do not matter; what is important is that, when the time arrives to perform, you feel confident and can concentrate on delivering your own performance.

Staging formats

In Unit 1 of your AS course, you will have explored two contrasting plays and written an evaluation of a live theatre performance. Part of the content of your Exploration Notes will have considered the visual, aural and spatial elements of production, and your theatre evaluation will have addressed a range of production values.

You will need to consider quite early during your development of the work what production, visual and spatial values you wish to achieve, and this will largely depend upon where you stage your performance. You will need to liaise with your teachers to make sure that you can gain access to any space for the later rehearsals, technical runs and performances. You may, however, decide that you would like to use another venue and this, of course, will depend upon what is available. Some work can be 'site-specific'; this means that it is designed for a particular space and this will influence how the piece develops.

There are many staging formats you can use and all of them will have an impact on the audience/performer relationship.

Key terms

proscenium arch
end-on staging
thrust staging
horseshoe staging
in-the-round staging
avenue staging
space-staging
promenade staging

- Conventional **proscenium arch** or **end-on staging** means that you will be separated from the audience, and will have to make sure that 'sight lines' are clear.

- If you adopt a **thrust** or **horseshoe staging** configuration, the event will be more intimate and the audience possibly more involved.

- **In-the-round** and **avenue staging** make demands on the performers to ensure that all the audience members see and hear effectively; also the use of furniture or set properties is more difficult with this choice. (The group in Case study 5 (page 49) uses an interesting layout that does, in fact, cause some problems that have to be addressed.)

- With **space-staging**, where the action happens amongst the audience, you can achieve a sense of intimidation, but making sure everyone can see is a challenge.

- If you use a **promenade** format, where the audience moves to different performance spaces within a venue, you will need to make sure that you have organised how you will guide and control the audience. The choice will depend on what effect you want to create and the resources available.

The case studies address some of the different staging layouts and will show you what is possible. Pages 147–152 of the AS Student Book provide details of the various types of performance space.

Key terms

set
lantern
cue

Design

If you are a design candidate, you will first need to decide which area of design you wish to specialise in: **set** design, lighting design, make-up, sound or costume design. All design decisions will depend on the type of performance that emerges, and you must be fully involved with the group to accommodate the decisions that occur during the creative process.

There are some excellent textbooks on areas of design in the theatre, and you should read as many of these as possible before you embark on the design for your group.

As a designer, you will need to understand and demonstrate how and why the design elements you create make the work more effective for the audience and help the actors on stage.

The table below shows the fundamental design elements that should be included; you can use this as a checklist to make sure that you have covered the essential requirements in relation to your design objectives.

Lighting	Set/props	Costume	Mask/make-up	Sound
Research and sketches showing the development of ideas.	Research and sketches showing the development of set/props ideas.	Research and sketches showing the development of costume ideas.	Research and sketches showing the development of ideas for masks/make-up.	Notes of the sound requirements for the work and initial ideas.
Justification for the final design decisions including: • **lantern** choice • angles/direction • intensity • speed • colour • key lighting • use of specials.	Justification for the final design decisions.	Justification for the final design decisions.	Justification for the final design decisions.	Justification for the final selection of sound.
The final lighting design, including the rigging plan showing lantern positions. You should aim to use at least three types of lantern.	A scaled ground plan and elevations for the final design in relation to the performance space.	Patterns for at least one costume and details of fabrics/materials.	Designs for at least three character masks and/or make-up charts for the production.	A source sheet for the creation of at least three original sound effects and sources for the remaining sounds.
A lighting plot and **cue** sheet.	A scale model of the final design in relation to the performance space.	A costume/accessories plot for the production indicating changes.	Provide details of materials and construction/application methods.	A cue sheet showing the position, length and output level of each cue.
The student must supervise the rigging, focusing and operation of the design within the production.	The student must supervise the construction, painting, hiring and/or finding of scenic elements to realise the design within the production.	The student must supervise the construction, buying, hiring and/or finding of the costumes and must demonstrate their use within the production.	The student must supervise the construction of the masks and/or application of make-up, and organise their use within the production.	The student must create the final sound track to include live and sampled material, and supervise its operation within the production.

It is important that all aspects of the research and preparation are developed individually. In addition, you must supervise the rest of the group in the practical execution of your designs.

You will need to discuss with your teachers what materials are available or what budget you have – if any! Design does not have to be complicated to be effective: you can create some impressive effects with a range of bought or found materials. If your final design is not achievable, you will need to provide an alternative and explain carefully in your evaluation why the finished product is not what you planned.

It is very important that you record the entire process. Do not 'clean up' your notes; you should include your early scribbles and sketches as these will often show how your design ideas progressed and developed.

Research will cover both the demands of the work as well as aspects of the design area, but make sure that you do not simply reproduce a lot of theory from the internet that is not related to your ideas. Any downloaded material must be used to show how your design ideas are being developed.

Tip

Make sure that what you design is achievable.

Directing

Within the total group number allowed (maximum of six), you may have a member who wants to offer directing as their individual skill rather than performing or designing. If this is your chosen skill, you will need to familiarise yourself with the demands of the role and research the skill.

Directing is a specialised skill, particularly when you are part of a group creating a piece of theatre. Managing other people, particularly actors, demands considerable tact, and the ability to be constructively critical without upsetting anyone.

There are a few books about the skill of directing, but these usually discuss the job in relation to the interpretation of existing plays. Some sections deal with encouraging the creativity of actors, but are still often very theoretical.

The director's work is most often based on a detailed study and analysis of the script to be produced. Many careful readings of the script help the director develop an individual vision of the playwright's intentions, which will form the basis of his or her interpretation. This sense of 'what the play is really about' will shape a director's thinking about every other aspect of the production. However, when working with a group who are creating the material, your task will be much more difficult and challenging.

The skill in directing group-created work relies on the ability to be the 'eyes and ears' of the group, advise on what is working and what is not, and suggest where improvements can be made. As director in *this* situation, you will need to take responsibility for ensuring that the group stays motivated and focused. You must also ensure that your performers undertake suitable warm-up activities, and that health and safety procedures are observed.

Keeping a record of the work as it develops is essential, and this would be one of the director's tasks. In the professional theatre, a director would usually have an assigned **stage manager** who would be responsible for maintaining 'the book'; this is the master copy from which the play will eventually be run during performances. The stage manager would enter all the director's instructions for specific moves, effects, staging, and so on. Often these would be in the form of small sketches showing key moments. As a director with a small group, you will need to record these key decisions for yourself.

Practitioner note

An interesting and useful book that recounts Max Stafford-Clark's experience of directing *The Recruiting Officer* is *Letters to George*, a detailed account of the rehearsal process he undertook in the form of a series of fictional letters to George Farquhar (who wrote the play in 1706). The book has been described as 'a candid insight into the rehearsal methods of one of the most respected and brilliant directors at work in the British theatre as well as an entertaining and instructive account of the state of the theatre.'

Below is a page from a typical script for the opening of *Macbeth*, annotated to show the positions and moves of the characters and a few of the lighting and sound cues that the director wanted.

ACT I	Blocking	LFX	SFX
SCENE I: A desert place		Lightning	
Thunder and lightning. -------------- --		-- Go	Thunder
Enter three Witches -------------- --			-- Go
	1st W enter US/ 2nd SL/3rd SR		
First Witch			
When shall we three meet again -------- --- Looking up at sky			
In thunder, lightning, or in rain?			
Second Witch			
When the hurlyburly's done, -------------- --- Gesturing SR to the battle			
When the battle's lost and won.			
Third Witch		Lightning	
That will be ere the set of sun. ----------- --- Pointing SL-------------------------		-- Go	Thunder
First Witch			
Where the place? -------------------------			-- Go
Second Witch			
Upon the heath. --------------------------- --- Looking off SL			
Third Witch			
There to meet with Macbeth. ------------- --- Looking into audience			
First Witch			
I come, Graymalkin! ---------------------- --- 1st exit DSL			
Second Witch			
Paddock calls. --------------------------- --- 2nd through audience			
Third Witch			
Anon. -------------------------------------- --- 3rd USR			
ALL			
Fair is foul, and foul is fair:			
Hover through the fog and filthy air.			
Exeunt			

Blocking refers to the positions, movements or gestures of the actor.
LFX is short for lighting effects and **SFX** sound effects DSL means 'downstage left' or towards the front of the stage on the left-hand side looking at the audience. USR means 'upstage right' or towards the back of the stage on the right-handside looking at the audience.

You can see that the director wants the battle to have been off stage right, and this is where Duncan, Malcolm, Donalbain and Lennox will enter in the next scene.

Many of the director's decisions will have been decided before the rehearsals begin, as they must develop a **vision** for the play and convey this to the cast. Many directors will then listen to the views of the cast as the actors begin to discover more about the characters; as a result, the vision may be modified or altered completely. The main point is that even in an 'organic' approach all decisions are conscious, even though some insights might occur by chance.

You *do not* need to produce a **prompt copy** like the one above, but your ideas about **staging**, patterns of movement, **audience focus**, **characterisation** and performance style must be clearly defined.

Further reading

You will find more detailed information on directing in the following books:

Mitchell, K., *The Director's Craft*.
Routledge, ISBN: 978-0415-40439-6

Mitter, S. and Shevtsova M., *Fifty Key Theatre Directors*.
Routledge, ISBN: 978-0-415-18732-9

Thorne, G., *Stage Design: A Practical Guide*.
Crowood Press, ISBN: 978-1861262578

Winslow, C., *Handbook of Set Design*.
Crowood Press, ISBN: 978-1861268136

Pilbrow, R., *Stage Lighting Design*.
Nick Hern Books, ISBN: 978-1854599964

[Various], *Scene Design and Stage Lighting*.
Wadsworth Publishing Co., ISBN: 978-0155061149

Key terms

vision
prompt copy
staging
audience focus
characterisation

Practitioner note

'So you get a kind of instinct of what you want to do. How you do it you often find out quite late in rehearsal. There is an instinct but the instinct is 'I want to do this'. The instinct about how to do it often comes through trial and error, quite late in the day.' Max Stafford-Clark, 2002 (© 2002 Nick Gibbs)

Checklist

The following chart will help you to make sure that you have covered all the essential areas in this unit both in your practical response and Supporting Written Evidence document.

	YES	NO
Have you made your choice as performer or designer clear?		
Have you confirmed the original stimulus/play?		
Does the group consist of between three and six members?		
Is the performance between 15 and 30 minutes in duration?		
Have you shown your original stimulus?		
Do your notes show how you researched the subject and theatrical practice?		
Do your notes give details of how the group worked on the piece and explored form, structure and style? In this section you should show how the work was developed, shaped and polished.		
Have you discussed in your notes how you developed your own role(s)?		
Do your notes make it clear who the target audience was?		
Have you showed how the work or ideas of a particular practitioner influenced the work?		
Do your notes show the impact of social, cultural and/or historical/political considerations on the audience?		
Have you made sure that the performance is recorded clearly and that you have identified all group members at the beginning of the recording?		
Have you completed an evaluation that appraises both the practical process and the success of the final product against your intentions for the work?		

CASE STUDIES

The case studies that follow show *some* of the possible approaches to the tasks. Within the six examples, there are groups who based their work on *existing plays*, some who worked on a particular *theme* and some who began with a photograph, article or object. Your teacher will decide the stimulus that you will respond to, and whilst it may be similar to one of the examples, it may be entirely different.

The studies are included to show how groups approach creating original material to perform; they also indicate where the groups have needed to engage in research and find out about performance or production techniques, and how they have recorded the process.

You must *not* think of the following as the only methods of creating original work: these are merely *possible* approaches.

You can view extracts from two of the pieces if your teacher has access to the *A2 Planning, Teaching and Assessment Guide*, as moments from Case studies 3 and 4 were recorded. For the rest, you will have to try to picture the finished product.

Case study 1 (based on articles about animals in zoos)

Charlotte's group: Charlotte, Erica, Mandy, Frances

Group background

Our group was made up of four girls studying A2 Drama and Theatre Studies in a state Specialist Performing Arts comprehensive school. All four of us took GCSE Drama and two of the girls did dance at A-level.

During our AS year, we studied *The Cherry Orchard* for Unit 1 and linked this to the work of Stanislavski. We also explored *Accidental Death of an Anarchist* alongside the work of Dario Fo, and had several workshops from visiting teachers; one of these was on *commedia dell'arte* and we made up a performance from some of the *lazzi* (pre-rehearsed comic action used in the *commedia*, around which plots could be created). For Unit 2, we presented a range of monologues and duologues from contemporary plays and a performance of *The Trial* by Stephen Berkoff.

We were not really into naturalistic plays and preferred more contemporary and exciting work. We had seen a range of plays from West End musicals to small-scale touring companies.

Our stimulus was a photograph and promotional literature about the adoption of animals in zoos.

Stage 1: Starting point

We were given the following picture and article as a starting point, and began by brainstorming our ideas on a large sheet of paper.

Kingdom of Gorillas

Animal Adoption not only makes a unique gift idea for yourself or someone special, it also makes a valid contribution to the running costs of Staunley Zoo and Farnley Zoo. Adopt any animal at either zoo from as little as £20.

Supporting on a level that is appropriate to you will make all the difference in the world. You'll receive a colour photograph of your adopted animal species as well as an adoption certificate, annual subscription to *Going Wild* magazine and an opportunity to visit the zoo. You may adopt any animal at Staunley Zoo and Farnley Zoo. Please contact us directly for more details.

After reading the article, our teacher only gave us two minutes to write any thoughts that came into our heads onto a large sheet of paper. The result is shown below.

Fancy dress	King Kong	Planet of the Apes	Tarzan	Sad eyes
Tea party	Circus	GORILLA	Role reversal	Banana
Loss of habitat	Engaged to an ape		Ape wins X Factor	

Key term

spontaneous improvisation

We knew from earlier work that we had to explore all the ideas that had been put down through **spontaneous improvisation**.

During the first session we tried out the following scenarios (the brackets show which idea they were based on):

- a scene in which humans were in cages and 'on display' for the entertainment of apes [Planet of the Apes]
- a party where no one is in fancy dress apart from one person dressed as a gorilla [fancy dress]
- a girl taking an ape home to meet her mum and dad [engaged to an ape]
- a group being terrorised by an escaped gorilla [King Kong]
- scientists arguing the merits of maintaining rainforest [loss of habitat]
- a gorillas' tea party [tea party]
- Tarzan being 'rescued' by an ape [Tarzan]
- inner monologue of a gorilla [sad eyes]
- a circus ape who was 'on strike' [circus]
- a gorilla on a TV chat show talking about his rise to stardom [*X Factor*]
- feeding gorillas at the zoo, and two gorillas talking about the merits of a banana diet [banana].

None of the ideas resulted in anything that we wanted to take further, but many of the improvisations were very funny and we had all enjoyed the work. At the end of the lesson, the teacher who had been observing and recording us suggested that we should continue to think about the initial stimulus and do some further research into the topic. We also agreed that the next session should start with us looking at the video of us working on our initial improvisations to see if anything was worth developing further.

Stage 2: Review of initial explorations

Our teacher started the session by showing us a sample of the practical work that we had engaged in during the last lesson, and pointed out that most of the results were comical.

We were then instructed to spend ten minutes only deciding four things:

1. What had been the most impressive piece of theatre we had seen together?

2. What style of performance did we most enjoy?

3. What impact did we want to create for an audience?

4. Who was our target audience?

After some discussion, we agreed on the following:

1. The piece of theatre that we remembered most was *Shockheaded Peter* by Cultural Industry and the Tiger Lillies at the Lyric Hammersmith.

2. The style of performance that we most enjoyed was:

   • fast moving

   • very physical

   • comical, but with some point

   • using grotesque, 'over the top' characters that were easily identifiable to any audience.

3. We wanted the audience to find the work enjoyable, but also to think about it afterwards and realise that there was a deeper meaning.

4. We wanted to perform to an audience of our parents and peers.

Our teacher then fed back to us the significance of both our practical exploration and decisions we had made about style and format.

It was very clear that we were not interested in creating a 'story' with realistic characters, but we did want the piece to make some sense. It was also clear that we were drawn very much towards a comical and very obviously 'theatrical' style of performance that would make the audience laugh.

We then remembered the earlier *commedia* workshop that we had done, and our teacher suggested that we should focus on archetypes we would like to create that would be instantly recognisable to the audience, could be comical and would offer opportunities for us to interact within the group and create comic contrasts.

Again, we used the brainstorm idea to create an initial list of characters that we could depict and create a range to 'fit' the group. The result is shown below.

Group of teachers	Mothers at a playgroup	Hippies
Colleagues in an office situation	Young children	Astronauts
Women at a Women's Institute (WI) meeting		
Shop staff	Athletes	

Our teacher then suggested that we should improvise by discussing the original article as if we were characters in the types listed above. Very quickly several of the categories were discarded as they did not allow us to talk about the subject. Astronauts, teachers, young children, athletes, office staff and mothers at a playgroup were rapidly rejected. When discussing the topic as 'hippies' some very amusing ideas were raised, but the characters that we created were very similar. When we 'became' characters at a WI meeting, we knew straight away that the scenario provided opportunities to exaggerate characteristics and genuinely create a range of grotesque personalities that could work together and lead to some strong moments of tension and humour.

By the end of the lesson, we had decided that we would research potential characters that might belong to the WI movement in a stereotypical manner, and that we would all think about possible situations that might involve the adoption of a gorilla.

Stage 3: Breakthrough

When we next met, the teacher fed back our decisions and suggested that we spend a few minutes either developing characters or discussing any research results. Since we had all researched the idea of WI women, we wanted to share our ideas, and so immediately began a lengthy discussion about possible scenarios that became increasingly improbable. The teacher then decided to intervene and gave us three situations to 'place' the characters in to see what might develop in terms of character.

The situations were:

1. Waiting for the arrival of the judges' results for a cake-making competition

2. On a car journey, but unsure of the directions

3. Putting up a tent on a windy day.

All three scenarios allowed us to explore ideas about possible characters and the relationships between them that were beginning to develop.

The results of the three improvisations confirmed that we wanted our piece to involve the four characters that we were developing, but we also wanted to multi-role and had still not clearly defined a situation in which to place the characters.

Towards the end of the lesson, the teacher asked us to brainstorm the original stimulus but 'in role' as our developing character. The result is shown below.

Feeding bananas	Visiting the adopted animal
Liberating our adopted gorilla	Being captured
On safari (came from the tent exercise)	Naming the gorilla

Unlike earlier sessions, we did not explore the ideas through improvisation, but instead immediately agreed that putting our characters in a militant scenario would generate comic potential. We decided that we would develop a situation in which the women had adopted a gorilla, and then having decided that it was cruel to keep the animal in a zoo, agreed to mount an 'undercover' operation to put up a large sign in the gorilla cage as a protest about keeping animals in cages. (One of the 'Hippie' improvisations had focused upon 'the freedom of all animals, man!')

As the characters became distinct, it was clear that they allowed great opportunities to create tension throughout the various sections. For example, Frances had created a rather timid character that was vague and forgetful; Mandy's character was dominant and bossy; Erica wanted to be in control and was always challenging the dominant character, and the last member (mine) was very highly strung and prone to attacks of hysteria.

The structure of the piece that quickly emerged was that the women would meet at an agreed rendezvous and 'check' that they were equipped for the operation ('Mission Impossible' style). The next section would be the journey to the zoo (based on our earlier exercise of being lost in the car). The next section would be the women 'breaking into' the zoo and one of the team accidentally leaving the door open.

We ran through this story line adding and altering dialogue as ideas were generated through the improvisation. We made sure that the work was videoed so that we could choose the best moments to polish.

At this point we could not think of a suitable ending and felt that the start was too abrupt, so decided to think about the other issues before the next lesson.

Stage 4: Reviewing the structure

After a brief warm-up run by our teacher, we watched the practical work from last session and were instructed to run through the ideas that we had created so far. This helped us cement the ideas and characters firmly, and allowed time for further exploration and development.

Our teacher suggested that we should consider several theatrical devices to see if any would generate ideas for the introductory scene and a suitable ending. Within the list (see conventions on page 10) we discussed possible techniques that we had used before, and felt that it would be a good idea to start the piece at the end and use a flashback technique to show how the characters had arrived at that moment.

Some discussion followed about how to make it clear to the audience that the events being shown were from an earlier moment in time. We had agreed that we did not want to rely on technical effects such as **fade**-outs to achieve our aim, and so we began to explore a range of approaches. It was agreed that we would begin the piece as TV and radio news crews reporting the strange events at the zoo and the fact that a large gorilla had been released. This would allow us to adopt other roles, and to ensure that this was as high energy as possible, we decided to use overlapping dialogue focusing on key phrases but repeated in pseudo foreign languages (this came from an early workshop on *Top Girls*).

The piece would now begin with frenetic snippets of information in German, Italian, French and Russian (with English phrases mixed in) that conveyed the outcomes of the WI women's exploits without offering any real details. To achieve the flashback effect, we made the reporters' voices fainter as they walked backwards from the audience into the shadows upstage where we would put on our clothing items to denote our WI characters.

We were able to use the gibberish reporters' scene to end the piece, but still had not decided what should happen after the women realised that they had mistakenly released the gorilla. Since one of our earlier brainstorm ideas had been about reversal of roles, we talked about ending with the gorilla outside the cage looking in at the women, but with only four in the group this was not possible. Also, we did not want to become involved in any representation of the gorilla through costume or otherwise.

The solution, though bizarre, emerged from the character of one of the women who, upon realising that they had let the gorilla free, commented that the children would be so disappointed not to see him and give him his bananas. From this 'in role' observation, we decided on the scenario that the ladies would have to act like gorillas so that the children would not be disappointed.

Since the final moments of the 'story' now had us acting as gorillas, still with respective WI traits, we had to decide how to return to the news reporters. This was achieved through a gradual morphing physically and vocally from WI gorilla to reporter. The sound bites continued to overlap until a key moment when in unison we decided on the phrase 'No comment!' followed by a **blackout**.

In terms of staging, we only used a low-level scaffold pole in front of the audience to suggest a zoo-like barrier, and upstage we had a series of vertical bars that we could squeeze through. The rest of the stage was empty, and all the locations were created by the movements of the performers. The car, for example, was presented by us standing in a slightly fanned out formation so that all the women's reactions could be viewed clearly.

Our characters were very stereotypical and exaggerated for comic effect, and the vocal and physical pace of the work was highly energised and maintained throughout. The situation was completely bizarre, but we made sure it was very polished and hoped that the audience's reaction would be positive.

Key terms

fade
blackout

Stage 5: Polishing to performance standard

The remaining sessions were used to develop the basic outline, often through character interactions, ensure that our characteristions were secure, and polish the work until we achieved the necessary level of pace. During this process, we recorded the work at regular intervals to make sure that the audience focus was clear and that comic moments were highlighted through the correct delivery of dialogue or physical action. We also previewed the work at various stages to other senior students and teachers.

There were moments when this stage of the work became tedious, but we used a variety of rehearsal techniques to maintain our enthusiasm, and these sometimes led to interesting developments of character and/or plot. For example, running the piece as Super Heroes was great fun and helped develop the grotesque nature of the women. Similarly, a rehearsal conducted entirely in mime added effective moments to the physical aspects of the 'clandestine entry' scene.

One aspect of the work still worried us because we had always wanted to make sure that, even though the piece was bizarre and amusing, the central question of whether animals should be in zoos would still emerge.

To address this, we went back to one observation from our initial brainstorm sheet where the words 'sad eyes' had been written by Mandy. Despite our reluctance to use technology, we decided to black out on the reporters and then freeze their positions, whilst a large projected image of the gorilla would be shown looking out at the audience. This in turn would slowly fade, leaving the eyes until the last moment. We all liked this idea, so we then spent some time making sure that the image could be projected very large, and fade slowly.

Throughout the process we had all kept individual records of the research we had done. This included notes on the methods we used to create ideas, and also the styles of performance such as 'grotesque' characters and physical theatre techniques that we used.

We also had to evaluate the whole project and question if the process was as effective as it could have been, and whether we achieved our original aim. Some of the audience members' responses were included in this, but the main part was personal observations. As part of the evaluation, we had to describe the finished product and my definition was as follows:

'We created a very physical style of work with high levels of energy and pace that used larger than life characters placed in a very surreal, *commedia-*influenced, situation. It was intended to be very entertaining and amusing for the audience, but at the end we wanted the audience to be left wondering about the morality of caging animals as they gazed into the sad eyes of the animal on screen.'

Case study 2 (based on articles about immigration and 'teacher-in-role' improvisation)

Peter's group: Kyra, Alex, Susan, Tom, Kevin (lighting), Jasmine (costume)

Group background

We were a group of three boys and three girls at a community college. We all took GCSE Drama and decided to continue with the subject at A-level. Two members of the group were interested in design and lighting, but Jasmine also performed in the piece.

For Unit 1 in our AS year, we spent a lot of time looking at Stanislavski and his ideas about creating believable characters on stage. We also looked at the ideas of Brecht and how his plays did not always rely on creating 'real' characters. We studied *The Cherry Orchard* and *Our Country's Good*, linked to each practitioner, through workshop sessions, and performed extracts from both plays.

For Unit 2, we decided to stage a performance of *Blue Remembered Hills*. We also presented a series of monologues and duologues based on the theme of childhood as an evening performance for friends and family.

During the first year of the course, we had several visiting workshops on physical theatre, mime and creating character, and visited several professional productions of both traditional and very modern devised theatre.

Stage 1: Starting point

We were given extracts to read from two articles about the issue of immigration; one was from *Mail Online*, and the other was from *The Independent on Sunday*. The articles were given out in the previous lesson, and we were told to prepare a short summary of what we had read in each.

Immigration timebomb:

Lies that created a soaring population

Ten years of complacency. Ten years of dishonesty and drift. Ten years in which Britain has been sleepwalking into a social revolution. No longer is it possible to pretend that Labour's failure to tackle immigration isn't having the most profound consequences. A devastating analysis by Cambridge economics professor Robert Rowthorn warns that our population will soar to 81 million within the next 70 years, largely because of immigration and a higher birthrate among immigrant families.

His findings echo projections by Oxford professor David Coleman, which show the number living here will rise to at least 75 million within 40 years. That will impose huge pressures on public services. The increase will be the equivalent of two cities the size of London, with all that means for the green belt, water supplies and the environment. Our ethnic mix will be transformed, with non-whites making up 29 per cent of the population, compared with nine per cent at the last census. A revolution, indeed.

Yes, past immigration has brought considerable advantages. Public services couldn't function without staff from overseas. And as this paper has frequently argued, properly managed migration can have great economic benefits, as the American experience shows.

But there isn't a trace of proper management in a Government that has lost control of our borders, allowed the asylum system to slide into a shambles and presided over the biggest surge of immigration in our history, while massaging the figures to hide the truth. Far from consulting the public, it stifled discussion (until recently) by smearing critics as "racist".

Whatever their colour or creed, the people of Britain deserve better than this. We need open, honest debate. Shouldn't Labour begin by publishing a sober assessment of how many more people this small island can absorb?

Malicious, misguided, and badly misinformed

The House of Lords economic committee's report on immigration styles itself as an impartial and dispassionate statistical analysis and claims that such questions as the impact of migration on "cultural diversity and social cohesion…are outside the scope of our enquiry". This is a study which purports to stick to the hard economics.

If only it did. The report has been delivered with some staggering anti-immigration spin. Every statistical study that seems to suggest the negative effect of migrants has been emphasized and every piece of evidence that suggests a positive impact has been played down. It should also be noted that the conclusions of the report seem designed to bolster the Conservatives' policy of putting a cap on immigration from outside the EU. Perhaps that is not surprising given the background of some of the peers on the committee. But let us concentrate, rather, on what the report actually says.

First the methodology. The report insists that GDP growth is a "misleading criterion for assessing the economic impacts of immigration on the UK".

Is it? Presumably the report's authors would not suggest ignoring GDP growth rates when it comes to measuring national economic health. So why does overall GDP suddenly become such a "misleading" indicator when it comes to analyzing the economic impact of immigration? The suspicion must be that this is because GDP figures show, unequivocally, that immigration has boosted our national economic performance. … The truth is that immigration has been of great economic benefit in recent years. Our public services, construction industry, agriculture and retailers rely to a considerable extent on immigrant labour. Immigrants teach in our schools, care for the elderly and pick our fruit. And despite the assertions of this report, there is little reason to believe the domestic workforce would be able to fill all these gaps. The NHS, for instance, would almost certainly collapse without migrant labour.

In short, we would all be worse off without the hard work of immigrants. To label this contribution "small" is not only economically dubious; many will find it downright insulting.

At the start of the lesson, we were ready to offer our thoughts on the two extracts we had read, but the teacher began the lesson by setting a scene and immediately entering in role. The scenario was as follows:

Place: biscuit factory canteen.

Roles: workers at lunch break.

Situation: a relative of mine had been turned down for a job and told that there were no vacancies.

Into this situation the teacher arrived (in role as a new Eastern European worker) and asked in very broken English if she could join our group. She then began to complain about the conditions in the factory, and in particular the poor quality of the canteen food.

The improvisation that followed was difficult, because even though we were used to the method of teacher in role, we wanted to attack her attitude, but our British reserve held us back. When she left the improvisation to speak to the boss about her concerns, we really began to say what we thought about her (in character), and decided that as a group we would 'take action' about a foreigner being hired over our own relatives.

After a while, we began to organise a strike meeting, and the teacher returned (in role now as our employer) to question what we were doing. She implied that the company had agreed a policy of employing foreign workers as they were more reliable and willing to work for lower wages. Later, when she again returned as the new employee, we informed her that she was not earning the same money, but she claimed that she was quite happy with her pay.

After the teacher left the improvisation, we had a new topic of concern which was the fact that eventually we would have to work for the same lower wage as the new employee.

At the end of the lesson, the teacher asked us to discuss what had happened in the improvisation, and how we felt about the situation. She also suggested that we should consider what we had read in the two articles and think about whether our views had changed at all.

After a very lively discussion, we decided that a lot of what the papers reported was for sensationalism, just to sell their paper, and that there were a lot of unfounded objections to the whole idea of immigrants.

At the end of the lesson, we had arrived at two potential topics for our work: a piece that tried to show how the media twist events to sell papers, and the phobic response to the number of Eastern European immigrants.

Since we could not decide immediately on the focus for our work, the teacher suggested that we research both ideas and bring the results to the next lesson.

Stage 2: Decision time

When we arrived at the next lesson, nobody had really done very much research and we did not know where to go with the work. Fortunately, our teacher had anticipated our lack of input and had brought in the play *Émigrés* by Slawomir Mrozek.

We read the play, watched part of a documentary about immigration and decided that we wanted to explore how it must feel for an immigrant in a strange country when they do not speak the language very well and have very few possessions.

The next decision was about the style of the piece, and whether we should attempt realism or try to generate feelings in the audience through a more stylised form of performance. Alongside this was the decision to target the work at an audience of adults, made up of our parents and any other adults we could persuade to come to the performance.

As we could not decide, our teacher set us a practical task:

- We had to use the lesson to create a scene where a group of new immigrants has landed in England by boat, and develop the dialogue between them and the immigration officer who is trying to decide whether they should be allowed to enter the country.

- From the improvisation, we had to write a script that sounded realistic.

We set to work and soon created a scene that contained misunderstandings, anxiety and threats. We then sat down to write the script as a group with one of the team writing and everyone offering suggestions.

When it was complete, the teacher photocopied the three pages and instructed us to rehearse the scene as she was going to record the result.

This was done, and after a short cool down session, the lesson ended.

The next lesson began with our teacher showing us the short scripted piece that we had rehearsed the previous lesson. As soon as we had seen the work, we all wanted to change bits of the dialogue, and agreed that the scene did not seem natural. Our teacher explained that the exercise was to make us aware of the time it would take to create an entire piece if we intended to opt for realism. She reminded us of the plays we had seen during the year, both on stage and on video, such as *The Street of Crocodiles* by Théâtre de Complicité. The realisation of the time needed to write effectively decided us, and we all agreed that we would use a combination of stylised performance and naturalistic dialogue.

Kyra suggested that a narrator would be a good method of 'stringing' the moments together, and we all agreed that this would make the work flow more easily. However, we still did not have a storyline and this was our next priority.

After discussion, we agreed that we wanted to make the audience feel sympathetic towards the problems faced by immigrants rather than hostile towards them. We spent the rest of the lesson discussing possible plot lines, and eventually ended up with the following:

Scene 1:	Montage of news reports telling of the persecution of an ethnic minority [nonspecific] and atrocities being carried out. [Harsh white lights flashing like cameras]
Scene 2:	A family hiding and trying to decide what possessions they could carry. [Sepia lighting]
Scene 3:	A representation of a very difficult and dangerous journey. [Blue wash and haze]
Scene 4:	Arrival in a foreign land. [Sepia]
Scene 5:	The struggle to get recognition – work and a place to stay. [Sepia with pools of light for the private thoughts section]
Scene 6:	The decision – to stay or move on again? [Blue wash]

We knew that we would not try to create a realistic play with a linear plot line and sequence of events, but having a secure shape for the work allowed us to experiment with different ways of showing the events within each scene.

Kevin had decided from the start that he wanted to design and operate the lighting, and he suggested that part of his role could be the creation of a montage of images and clips to project during the first scene. Everyone agreed that this was a good idea, and he began to search for material. As we were going to perform the first scene in front of these images, we agreed that it should be a movement sequence with disjointed moments of dialogue that created the sense of being hounded without trying to create realistic dialogue.

To create a sense of confusion, we individually decided on words and short phrases that we would use in a random order overlapping each other. This would happen at the same time as the movement sequence and the back projection to create a sense of confusion and panic.

Susan had done dance lessons for years, and agreed to work out a series of moves based on contact, lifts and pressure that the boys would feel happy with as they had not much dance experience. Working on this sequence to make sure that it could be very fast and furious, but at the same time safe, took most of the session and we made sure that our teacher filmed it as this was a good example of us working in a practical way.

Stage 3: Development

When we arrived for the next session, Kevin had put together a sequence of slides and moving images with a soundtrack of warfare mixed up with heavy metal tracks, all overlapping and very unclear. We thought it sounded and looked great, and we quickly shaped our movement work to the audiovisual sequence. Opening done!

We then went straight into improvisation of a scene where the family members were trying to decide what possessions they could take with them when they leave their country. The only decision we made before starting was the allocation of characters as below:

Me [Kyra]:	Mother
Alex:	Father
Tom:	Grandfather
Jasmine:	My sister
Susan:	Grandmother

We used spontaneous improvisation, and simply kept the action moving by responding to each other in character.

Kevin (lighting) watched the improvisation, and made notes about the parts that seemed to be effective. He also suggested that it would be a good idea to put pressure on the group in this scene by having noises off stage as if a search party was moving from house to house. Everyone agreed that this would add tension to the situation. We also decided that we would have occasional off-stage noises of gunshots and distant explosions to maintain the idea of this being a war-torn country.

The remainder of the session was spent discussing what had developed in the improvisation, and rerunning moments to get the best structure and make sure that the dialogue was convincing.

We next wanted to create the family's journey, but we did not want it to be realistic. Our teacher suggested we look back at the workshop exercises we had done in the first year for the AS course. Tom suggested that we could use the idea of a series of freeze-frames, and make each still picture a representation of the dangers of the journey. We liked this idea and started to create a series of images.

Kevin thought that it would be a good idea if we used lighting to suggest a camera flash for each picture. Alex suggested that we could actually take digital pictures of ourselves, and these could be added in sequence to the backdrop to create a montage of what has just happened on stage. This proved very difficult because the projections could not happen in 'real time' and the pictures would have to be taken before the performance. This meant that we had to make sure that we were always in the same position as the picture, and that our costumes would also be the same. We liked the idea though, and decided to use it. The rest of the session was spent deciding on 15 freeze-frames to show the journey. This decision gave Kevin another task to add to his growing list of duties.

The next scene we had to create was the arrival in another country. We agreed that we needed some humour in the piece, and that this could be achieved through the idea of not being able to understand what people are saying, and doing the opposite of what was asked for.

During the lesson, we tried out lots of possible scenes including working out which underground train to use, ordering a meal in a café, shopping in a large supermarket, asking for directions, filling in a benefit form, and a parent / teacher meeting.

We had great fun with the improvisations, but when we watched them, we decided that the humour actually did not fit in with the other scenes and that we wanted to suggest real confusion rather than a comic situation. We also agreed that we liked the idea of trying to get somewhere, and the confusion that the underground can create. So we decided to work on an abstract movement scene in which the family attempt to find out which train to take and are not really helped by other people.

We liked the sequence when it was complete, but decided that we needed to find a suitable piece of music that could help convey the sense of confusion the family felt. We all agreed to look for suitable music and bring these to the next session. We actually had some private study time, so we spent this looking for the right music and finally settled on a piece we found on the internet called 'Medicine Man' by The Residents. This was a suitably strange and fragmented piece that reflected what was happening to the characters at that moment.

During the next lesson, we improvised the family at home with the male members arriving and explaining that they had been unable to get any work despite having good qualifications and experience in different professions. This did not work very well because, when we tried to talk about how qualified we were, we lacked the factual knowledge to make it sound real.

We spent the rest of the lesson agreeing what skills/trades we each had, and agreed to research our job for the next meeting. We came up with the following trades/professions:

Me [Kyra]:	Mother	Housewife good at cleaning and laundry
Alex:	Father	Electrician
Susan:	Grandmother	Housewife
Tom:	Grandfather	Retired from printing
Jasmine:	My sister	Typist

Research into each of the different occupations was very important, and when we returned for the next session, we were all able to talk about our work in a more convincing way. This research became part of our Supporting Written Evidence document.

We then discussed how we could get across the idea of being unsuccessful without taking it in turns or making it too obvious through the dialogue. As the work was developing, we found that we were happier with the moments that were not entirely naturalistic, and thought we might present this section in a stylised way.

Our teacher reminded us of the idea of thought-tracking to show the difference between what characters are saying and their inner thoughts. We tried the scene again with one member of the group calling 'freeze' at various points. At that point everyone on stage would freeze, apart from the person speaking, who would address the audience directly to tell them what they were really thinking.

When we watched the recording of the scene, we all agreed that the idea was effective, but that it was too even and predictable. After some discussion, we agreed on a range of short and long direct addresses that would make the intention clear, but keep the section sharp and precise.

The last section was the most difficult, because we had to convey the very complicated decision-making that the family had to go through without the creation of lengthy scripted dialogue.

Susan suggested that we could each tell our own version of the event as a flashback in the past tense. Her monologue began: 'When the decision was agreed that we would return to our home, I was overjoyed until I remembered how difficult the journey had been.' Tom's began: 'We heard the killing was over from the BBC news.'

As we did not want to recreate naturalistic dialogue, we agreed that we would have three or four phrases each, and that these would be overlapped to create a montage effect of thoughts and feelings. We experimented with lots of runs until we arrived at a sharp and effective sequence.

The final problem we were faced with was how to end the piece in a way that would leave the audience thinking about the subject and the issues involved. The use of projected statistics was suggested, but we did not want the work to end like a lecture.

Jasmine said we should end with a series of frozen images that showed what the family had been through, and this should be underscored by music. Her idea was to fade the lighting and music very slowly at the end to create a sad effect. We all thought this was a good idea, and agreed to look for a piece of suitable music.

We all arrived at the next session with CDs that we thought might be suitable, and after about 30 minutes of listening had narrowed the choice down to two. Some of the group liked 'Bad World' by Michael Andrews, and others preferred 'Run' by Amy McDonald. We thought that the best way to make the final decision was to run the scene twice using each piece of music, and look at the recorded results. Having done this, we finally agreed that we would use 'Bad World'.

The last task for us when we had the music was to work out the series of still images that showed the family leaving and returning. We created a sequence, but when we watched it on video, we did not think that it was clear what was happening. After experimenting with several ideas, we decided to combine the phrases from the scene before with appropriate frozen images. As the phrases were repeated, the images accompanied them and the music faded in as the dialogue got quieter. When we watched the sequence, we agreed that it was much stronger and clearer for the audience.

Stage 4: Polishing the work

All we had to do now was run the performance lots of times to polish the work so that we felt confident that nothing would go wrong, and that we could maintain our characters and the pace of the work. We also had to get used to our costumes that Jasmine had created. She had found lots of drab clothes that looked as if they were 'hand-me-downs' and we had a session trying on what she suggested, and moving around the stage so the rest of the group could comment. The older characters felt that having the right clothing really helped them with their characters. We filmed the production twice, and spent some time making sure that all the transitions between scenes were smooth and that the different styles blended together as we did not want the audience to 'see the joins'.

We also had to think about the lighting and sound, because we wanted the stylised scenes to appear hazy and dreamlike. Kevin had been part of all the development, and had clear ideas about what he wanted to show. He suggested that we should use a haze effect for the non-realistic moments with a blue wash and a sepia effect for the naturalistic scenes. When he showed us what they looked like, we all agreed that the 'real time' scenes would be in a yellowy wash and the stylised scenes in blue. We filmed it again with the lighting and sound, and were satisfied with the finished piece as we felt it showed some aspects of the problems that asylum seekers face.

Case study 3 (using a play as the stimulus)

Mark's group: Mark, David, Stephen, Natalie

Group background

We were a small group of three boys and one girl at a private school, all interested in performing. We had worked together since we did GCSE Drama in Year 11.

For Unit 1 in our AS year, we studied *The Good Person of Szechwan* and linked this to the ideas of Bertolt Brecht, and also the ideas of Peter Brook alongside the play *The Marat Sade*.

For Unit 2, we presented monologues and duologues from plays by Harold Pinter and Samuel Beckett, and a shortened version of *The Fire Raisers* by Max Frisch within a larger group.

This case study performance was recorded and can be viewed on the A2 Planning, Teaching and Assessment Guide, if your teacher has this.

Stage 1: Starting point

When we arrived to begin Unit 3, our teacher explained that we had to create an original piece of work based on a given stimulus, a theme or an existing play, and gave us the choice of our starting point. After a short discussion, we agreed that since we had enjoyed working on *The Fire Raisers* for Unit 2, we would like to adapt an established play in a similar style.

Our teacher accepted our decision, and then offered advice to help us choose a suitable play. We were warned:

- not to try and repeat earlier work
- not to choose any play because of the number of parts
- to select plays that were well regarded and allowed us to focus on specific aspects
- to be careful with unknown authors and plays on the internet
- to select plays that offered opportunities to show our range of performance techniques
- to avoid GCSE texts and children's plays.

We were then taken to the resource centre, and guided to the works of playwrights we had looked at during our AS studies.

Nothing immediately appealed to everyone in the group. Our teacher warned us about the danger of taking a long time to find a suitable play, and that every week spent looking shortened the time we had to work on our choice. We all agreed that we would only spend the time until our next lesson finding a play; we also agreed that if we failed to agree on a play, we would accept the teacher's selection.

Stage 2: Selecting a text

We all found plays that we thought might be good to work on, and in the next lesson took turns to explain our choice. Mark had found *The Pitchfork Disney*, and when we read it we all thought the dialogue was sharp and witty. Also, as some of us wanted to present comedy, and others more serious work, we thought that the absurd nature of this play had a bit of each. We also thought that the play had many aspects that we could concentrate on.

After reading the play through as a group, we quickly realised that the character of Pitchfork comes in quite late in the play without any dialogue, and that this would not give one of our group enough to do in the play. As there was only one female character, it was not an option to alter much in this role, but because her twin, Presley, has such rapid and extreme mood swings, we decided we could show him as a schizophrenic played by two of the boys. We liked this idea a lot, and found that it opened up a new interpretation of the play that we decided to explore.

It was fortunate that all the members of the group wanted to play certain roles, and there were no clashes. As Mark and David look similar, it was an obvious choice for them to play Presley between them. This was a logical interpretation, because it was clear from the dialogue that neither the brother nor sister in the play can function in society in a normal manner. Stephen wanted to play Cosmo Disney, and had an idea of how he wanted the character to appear; as there was only one female role (Hayley), this part was obviously for me.

Stage 3: First explorations

For the first exploration of this idea, we tried to divide the lines between the two characters playing Presley so that one had the angry or bitter lines, and the other the more caring and sympathetic dialogue. This proved very difficult as it was not possible to make one character angry all the time without altering many of the lines, and we did not want to do this. In the end, we decided that both the boys would adopt similar mannerisms and movements, and that one would tend to be more angry than the other without completely rewriting the dialogue.

Most of the next two sessions were spent editing the text to focus on the ideas that we wanted to convey to the audience. We all agreed that we should aim the work at an adult audience because some of the content was difficult to appreciate and we wanted them to find the characters of the twins amusing, but at the same time feel sorry for them, because they cannot function normally. We all agreed that the idea of the brother and sister living on a diet of chocolates and barbiturates was essential to highlight the inadequacy. The mysterious disappearance of 'Mummy and Daddy', who they fondly remember, is never explained; as we agreed that this was not essential to our view of the play, we decided to start with the twins arguing about whose turn it was to go shopping for chocolate.

With Disney's character, we wanted to make the audience feel nauseated by his vomiting on stage, and his eating of cockroaches as a cabaret act. Stephen also wanted to add some of the intimidating aspects of Pitchfork's character so that the audience would feel frightened for the brother and sister.

Many of the long emotional soliloquies by Presley could not be included because of the time limitations that the exam imposed, but we still wanted to show some aspects of the way that the twins exist by retelling stories and their nightmares, and the rather strange 'ritualistic' dialogue that they use. We also wanted to retain the fragmented feeling that was created by the text, so that the audience would never be sure what was real and what was imagined by the characters. The twins exist in a sort of 'dreamlike' state, and their only visitors are quite bizarre, and rather frightening, strangers.

Sorting out the script took us a long time, but we were also trying out the edits and discussing ideas about staging and character at the same time.

Stage 4: Staging the work

Once we had finalised the dialogue, we ran the piece a few times to see if it worked on stage, and then began to block in the moves. We had discussed the atmosphere that we wanted to create, and decided that the small studio space would be the best place to perform, as the audience would be close and the atmosphere very intimate.

All the action takes place in the twins' flat, and we agreed that we did not want to build a complete set but would use heaps of chocolate wrappers and sweets to show how they have been living. We thought this would be quite comic for the first part of the performance before Cosmo entered and changed the mood. Fortunately, Natalie's father worked for a chocolate distributor and was able to get us as much chocolate as we needed – not the easiest way to get through rehearsals with unlimited chocolate 'on tap'!

As Hayley sleeps so much, to escape from what might be lurking outside, it was essential that we had a bed as part of the set; we also needed a cabinet to 'store' the chocolates and biscuits.

The other very important part of the set was the door through which Cosmo bursts and is sick on the floor. The script suggested that this should have several locks on it, and at first we could not see how we could create this. However, when we started to walk the play through, we realised that the store cupboard stage left in the studio could be used. To suggest that Cosmo was entering from outside, we put a floodlight in the cupboard so that when he burst in, the light was behind him. We tried this out and agreed that it made a very dramatic entrance, and emphasised Hayley's paranoia.

One of the problems at this stage was trying to distinguish between the two boys playing the role of Presley. After quite a lot of experimentation and watching the results on video, we decided that they should try and develop similar mannerisms and movements, and that this, together with the same costume, should make the concept clear to the audience. We tested the work with fellow theatre studies students, and they said that they were a bit confused at the start, but soon realised that Hayley only ever addressed one at a time, and used the same name, and then it became clear that it was one person. This also worked with the bullying by Cosmo when he asks a follow-up question, but to the 'other' Presley.

Stage 5: Polishing the work

The next few sessions were spent working on the characters and interactions. The twins focused on developing the characteristics of 28-year-olds whose development had been arrested, and who lived in a terror of 'the outside'. They had to deliver the language in a young-sounding voice without becoming too 'childish'. It was difficult for Natalie as she spent a lot of the second half of the play asleep in a semi-drugged state. The character of Cosmo was so strange, with a mixture of menace, curiosity, frankness and extreme homophobia, that Stephen had to exaggerate his mannerisms and behaviour to make the character larger than life and unpleasant to the audience. He also adopted a staccato vocal delivery with long pauses to emphasise moments of intimidation or apprehension.

We ran the play many times, often exchanging lines between Mark and David to make sure that as far as possible they represented the sympathetic or more aggressive side of the character they played. These changes caused a few problems in the earlier rehearsals as the boys forgot who had agreed to deliver specific lines, but after several runs it became easier and more fluent.

It was agreed that the groups would assist in operating any technical aspects for each other, and as we kept these to a minimum the technical rehearsal was problem free.

To set the tone for the twins' dialogue and emphasise the fact that they had never really 'grown up', we decided to use a nursery rhyme tune, that sounded a little like an ice-cream van, to open and end the play. The lighting was very simple as we kept the same state throughout; even the cupboard light remained on.

We had a full technical/dress rehearsal for all the groups at our centre, and gave each other feedback. There were a few points made about the speed and delivery of the dialogue in some moments, and a few fellow students said that there were moments when they could not hear very well because they were too rushed or too quiet. We took these comments on board and spent the last few days trying to achieve more light and shade, and slow down the delivery so that significant moments would be effective.

We were satisfied with the final performance as we managed to both amuse and disturb the audience; we could hear the laughter and the groans when the nauseating moments happened. A few members also said that they felt very worried for the twins. The only aspect that we felt was not as effective as we had hoped was the **doubling** of Presley's character, as we did not feel that we focused enough on the two sides of his nature.

Key term

doubling

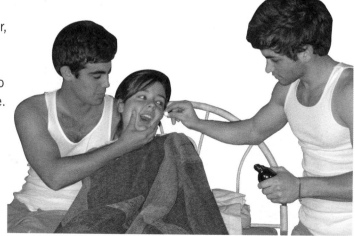

Case study 4 (using a play as the stimulus)

Joe's group: Joe, Phillip, Sean, Melissa

Group background

We were a group of three boys and one girl from a private school who all wanted to perform. We had known each other since Year 11, but not all of us had taken GCSE Drama.

For Unit 1 in our AS year, we studied *The Tempest* by Shakespeare and *The Trial* by Steven Berkoff, based on the story by Franz Kafka. For Unit 2, we presented monologues and duologues from a wide range of classical and modern plays, and a version of *Endgame* by Samuel Beckett.

Stage 1: Starting point

When we arrived to begin Unit 3, our teacher explained that we had to create a unique and original piece of drama, and gave us the choice of working from a stimulus, deciding upon a theme/issue or working from an existing play.

During our AS year, we had studied *The Tempest* by William Shakespeare and had enjoyed the practical work on the text. We had also taken part in a production of *Endgame* by Samuel Beckett and we thought it would be a challenge to work on a more modern play. We also wanted to work on a play with some substance to it. We therefore went to the school resource centre to find a text that inspired and allowed us to focus on some clear issues. We found several that we thought might be possible, and narrowed the choice down to four: *Cloud Nine* by Caryl Churchill; *Loot* by Joe Orton; *Death and the Maiden* by Ariel Dorfman; *The Straits* by Gregory Burke. After a lot of discussion, we decided to individually research the four plays and make a decision after we knew more about the choice.

When we met again, we were all quite excited with *The Straits*, and since it was about a group of teenagers, we thought it would be suited to our playing range. The cast was four young men and one girl, which also matched our group. We all thought that it was an exciting story line, particularly because of the controversy about the wars in Iraq and Afghanistan. We then read the play aloud and were a little worried about the strong language, the violence and the 'sex scene', but agreed that it would be challenging for us as actors.

This case study performance was recorded and can be viewed on the A2 Planning, Teaching and Assessment Guide, if your teacher has this.

Stage 2: Deciding a focus

The next decision was which aspects of the play we would focus on, and how we would treat the content in terms of performance style. The play deals with the 'coming of age' of four teenagers living on the Rock of Gibraltar in 1982 during a scorching season at the beach where they spend much of their time. The year is significant as it was during the Falklands War, and the older brother of 'Doink' is serving in the British navy in the war with Argentina.

The play focuses on the arrival of Darren on the island, and his emulation of Doink and his mate Jock, with much of the dialogue about fighting, killing and the enemy who Doink sees as the local population ('*spics*'). Darren's older sister, Tracy, is also part of the mix, and although she makes fun of Doink and Jock, she is attracted to the former and this leads to the sexual encounter that Darren interrupts.

Once everyone had read the play, a lengthy discussion followed about possible aspects that we could focus on. We agreed that we wanted to present the play in a naturalistic style, and use it to focus on the ideas of racism, sexism and bullying, both physical and mental, as this is what much of the play deals with.

Stage 3: Developing ideas

We spent the next few sessions paring the play down to the most basic plot line, and removing the wider story to focus on the relationships between the four young characters. We then spent a lot of time working on the different scenes to explore the inner motives of each of the characters, and decide what we wanted to convey to the audience at each point. Every scene was developed 'in action', in that we didn't sit and talk about what it should be like, but we tried out movements and character interaction even with scripts still not learned.

We discovered different aspects to the characters we were playing, and decided that, despite his 'big talk', the character of Doink was actually less prepared to get involved than he appeared. He was always egging others on to 'have a go', but never quite did himself. We agreed that at the end we wanted to show that despite the events in the play, he had not really changed, and was enjoying his ability to manipulate others.

Agreeing the focus for our version of the play took a long time, and there were regular debates about what a particular character was feeling at any given moment. Editing the script took several sessions, but this was an important stage as we needed to include the key moments that would allow us to show the tensions between the characters and convey the parallels between the war games of the boys and the British Empire. At one point, Tracy says to Darren "Watchin' soldiers and playin' soldiers. Is that all you and your mates can do?" Darren replies "Yep, that's about all, Sis." We all felt that this exchange summed up the lives of the three boys.

After about three sessions, we were happy that we had retained the essence of the play, but also developed a clear focus on the bullying that we wanted to show.

Stage 4: Staging the play

The blocking of the play was not preplanned, but emerged from the runs we did and the feedback from teachers and others in the class. We started to learn our lines as we experimented with different moves and gestures; at the same time, the relationships between the characters became clearer as we tried out a range of emotions and responses.

We were faced with a few issues that had to be tackled. One of these was the sex scene between Doink and Tracy. After a few experiments, usually accompanied by very unhelpful comments from the rest of the cast, and considerable amusement from all, we found a very easy solution as we decided that the couple could wrap themselves in the flag of St George that we used on stage as a symbol of the group's patriotism.

The second problem was the scene in which Doink kicks Darren in the face in a fit of anger. We knew that this had to be carefully choreographed so that it would be safe, but we also wanted it to look real. We talked to our dance teacher who spent a session with the two actors carefully staging the action. After lots of slow motion runs, they gradually speeded up the routine until it looked realistic. Darren fell facing upstage and held his hands in front of his face. Doink then kicked Darren's hands which made the right sound, and at the same time Darren bit into a blood capsule. The effect when he sat up facing the audience was amazing. When we ran the sequence for other members of the group, they all agreed that it looked totally realistic.

We carried on developing the characters and the interaction between them, often altering the emphasis or timing of the dialogue through constant monitoring by video and feedback from teachers. We were conscious of the amount of swearing in the play, and at first it felt very false as we would not normally use this language in the classroom. Our teacher explained that it would only feel natural when we stopped thinking about it and the lines became completely automatic. This proved to be the case, and after several rehearsals, we were not aware of the language as it felt natural for the characters.

Many of the following sessions were devoted to exploring the emotional relationships between the characters, and we looked again at Stanislavski's ideas about creating truthful characterisation. We analysed the characters to decide their objectives, and broke the scenes down into units that were given a specific purpose for each of the roles. We also looked at Stanislavski's ideas about tempo-rhythm to help us make the characters' behaviour as realistic and truthful as possible.

Many of the exercises and research that we did were included in our Supporting Written Evidence document, as so much of the success of the piece depended on achieving a sense of reality in the events on stage.

We had to decide how we were going to stage the play, as in the original script there were several different locations. Much of the action and dialogue that we used was set around the bay, where the boys spend time hunting octopuses, and the living room of Darren's house. We decided that we wanted a very sparse and representational set so we used just a sofa and a bed upstage for the indoor scenes, and set the outdoor scenes downstage. We decided that we could differentiate between the two areas through the use of stage lighting; very bright downstage to show the Mediterranean sun, and upstage muted straw lighting to give the impression of inside. We talked to the technical team who thought this was possible, and agreed that we would use the small studio space rather than the main theatre as we wanted to develop an intimate relationship with the audience through which they could feel the frustrations of the youngsters.

The other consideration was the opening and closing music, and we had a short session listening to music tracks to find something suitable. We eventually decided on a track by Moby called 'Flower' that had a strong bass beat.

Our teachers and peers thought that the finished piece was effective, and confirmed that they could feel the barely contained pressure and frustration that the group was experiencing. They also got the point about Doink as a bully who was himself afraid and inadequate. From our point of view, we enjoyed creating a realistic piece with some challenging emotional content.

Case study 5 (using a theme as the stimulus)

Estella's Group: Estella, Maxine, Stephanie, Aisha, Colette, Mia

Group background

We were a group of six girls at a rural comprehensive school. We had all taken GCSE Drama at the same school and wanted to continue with the subject at A-level so we were all very used to working as a team.

For Unit 1 in our AS year, we studied two plays about the effects of superstition and rumour, *Vinegar Tom* by Caryl Churchill and *Blood Wedding* by Frederico García Lorca. We also looked at the ideas of Antonin Artaud, Bertolt Brecht, Constantin Stanislavski and the theatre companies Trestle, Shared Experience and Théâtre de Complicite. For Unit 2, we performed a classical and modern monologue each and a version of *Lysistrata* in a very Brechtian style.

Stage 1: Starting point

Our teacher explained that for Unit 3 we had to create a unique and original piece of theatre, and that we could select one of the five themes below:

- Cardboard city
- A perfect 10
- Our planet
- The media circus
- The cult of celebrity.

We were told to split into pairs to discuss possibilities, and then report back to the whole group in ten minutes' time. I partnered Stephanie, and we both agreed that 'the cult of celebrity' idea with all the X Factor and Big Brother hype would be a popular choice, but we also thought that it might be a bit 'tacky' and an imitation of TV programmes. We rejected 'our planet' as being too obvious, as this topic had been very much in the news. We were not sure what 'cardboard city' meant and had to ask our teacher; we were told that in areas of London and other big cities, homeless people sometimes collected together and created shelters out of cardboard boxes. We thought this was a good subject to tackle, but were also quite interested in the idea of exploring how the media manipulate events to promote their own papers or programmes. We thought the 'perfect 10' idea would also be a possibility, as there had been a lot of news coverage about size zero models and women's attempts to look thinner.

After the ten minutes were up, we reconvened and shared our thoughts as a whole group. There was a lot of agreement in that none of the other pairs wanted to use the ideas of global warming or the cult of celebrity. Everyone was a little wary of the homeless topic, and we could not decide between the last two.

The teacher suggested that, before we made a final choice, we should research both topics and think about the sort of piece we wanted to create. In particular, he asked us to think about the impact on the audience; did we want to make a serious point, or did we want to make the point through a comedic approach?

Stage 2: Defining the focus

We discussed the project between lessons, and agreed that because there had been so much in the news about size zero models, we wanted to tackle the subjects of anorexia and bulimia. We also decided that we wanted to create a piece for a teenage audience and shock them using the methods suggested by Artaud. We then agreed that we would research the subject so that our factual content would be valid, and that we would think about Artaudian devices that we might use.

We agreed that we wanted to create a montage effect of fast movement, sound and images that would have a very strong impact on the audience.

During the next lesson, we explained our ideas to our teacher. He suggested that we should experiment with a range of music tracks to see what movements they suggested, look for images at the same time as we researched the topic, and try to establish a structure through which the aural/visual effects could be linked.

We agreed that we should provide a human focus for the audience, and that overall the work would try to convey the inner turmoil that a young girl suffering from anorexia experiences. At the same time, we wanted to show the pressures that society places on women to conform to a fashionable size and look.

We agreed that we did not want to tell a story in a linear manner, but wanted to bombard the audience with sights and sounds, and try to create an impact that would give them something to think about after the performance.

Our problem at this stage was that we knew the effect we wanted, but nothing concrete about how to achieve it. Our teacher suggested that we should begin with a list of all the aspects that we thought might be involved in this topic, and gave us five minutes to put down individual ideas on a large sheet of paper. The result is shown below.

Fashion shows	Models	Pressure to be attractive to men
Advertising	Trendy foods	Peer group pressure
Secrecy	Hiding the problem	Celebrity images	Depression

Stage 3: Developing ideas

As we wanted to bombard the audience with visual images and sound, we agreed that we would all look for music or images that we could use. Stephanie came the next week with a song by Jill Sobule called 'Supermodel' that had a very strong rhythm and perfect lyrics for what we wanted to explore, and we agreed that we would start with this music in the form of a fashion show. When we tried to create a 'catwalk' sequence, we could not decide where the platform should be in relation to the audience. We talked to our teacher who suggested that we should look again at the ideas of Artaud. After carrying out further research, we decided that we would use Artaud's ideas about performing in and around the audience, and agreed that we would create a cross with the audience in the corners (see page 51).

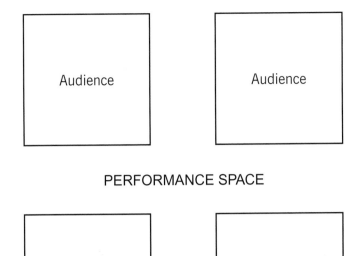

PERFORMANCE SPACE

This layout would enable us to use the aisles as catwalks, and also move behind and between the audience blocks.

The opening sequence involved us moving from all directions with very stereotypical model poses and walks, the song by Jill Sobule played very loudly, and the lighting changed colour and was interspersed with strobe flashes to imitate camera flashes.

Mia suggested that we should really shock the audience as soon as possible and put forward the idea that models are only viewed by those in the industry as cattle. She thought it would be shocking to link the idea of meat (cattle) to models always needing to shed weight by reaching through their clothes and bringing out handfuls of raw meat. We were all a little queasy at this idea, but liked the potential impact that it could achieve.

We asked our teacher what he thought about the idea and he confirmed that it was possible, but that we would need to warn any audience that the piece contained some disturbing images. We agreed to this, and experimented with the idea. It was a bit nauseating at first, but after a while we got used to it; however, we could not think of a way to stop the raw meat staining the costumes before we were ready. Mia finally came up with the idea that we could put cling film around our waists, then the meat, and then another layer of film. This worked well, as we had to rummage between the layers of cling film to get at the meat, which created the sense that we were tearing at the models' bodies.

The next thing we wanted to convey was the sense of isolation that young girls who have this illness often feel. We decided to do this through a voice-over soundscape of fragmented comments from family and friends all overlapping and not in any sequence. This soundtrack would suggest that everyone around the girl was concerned and supportive, but the movement sequence that went with it would show that she could not connect with anyone and that no one could get near to her. The main thing we wanted to avoid in this section was the idea of building the volume or pace to a crescendo that ended in a scream; this has been done so often by other groups that we thought it would be clichéd.

To create the people around the girl, we sat down and worked out what the relationship was and what attitude they had to her. From this, we decided what fragments of speech each could use. These were as follows:

It's a shame she's such a pretty girl.
[It's a shame. Such a pretty girl. Shame. Pretty girl.]

I keep telling her she's not fat, but it's no good.
[Not fat. No good.]

She's not happy and is always tired.
[Not happy. Always tired.]

I don't know why she wears those baggy clothes.
[Baggy clothes.]

She just won't eat.
[Won't eat.]

She doesn't socialise with friends.
[Doesn't socialise.]

The brackets show how the phrase was shortened during the sequence so that the words overlapped and became a jumble.

To achieve the effect we wanted, the rest of the group conveyed everyday activities such as crowds going to work, standing on buses and tube trains, drinking coffee, at work, in meetings, lunch breaks, and telling jokes. We experimented with these activities singly and in pairs and threes, watching each other to make a note of sequences that looked particularly good. Once we had created a bank of movements to choose from, we sat down and tried to structure them so the audience would be aware of what was happening. The patterns of movement were very repetitive and almost machine-like and the girl appears to bounce off each pair or group like a 'pinball'.

We were not sure how we should end the sequence, but through experimentation, the pace of the central girl's movement increased and became more agitated and frenetic. Towards the end, she stood in the middle of the cross and at a predetermined moment in the music, she fell backwards into the arms of two of the group, another pair immediately picked up her legs and we carried her off in a crucifix shape.

When we watched the sequence on video, we were pleased with the movements and vocal soundscape, but felt that it needed a musical underscore that could increase the tempo and add to the sense of pressure building within the girl. We all agreed to look for suitable music tracks that might create the effect we wanted. Everyone brought in a track that they thought would be suitable, and after listening to them all, we agreed on 'The Look' by Roxette as the lyrics were appropriate, and it had the right rhythm for the sequence we had planned without the need to make any alterations.

One of the most common aspects of the illness that we discovered from our research was the fact that sufferers become very secretive and try to hide their actions, particularly if family and friends are trying to keep a watch on them and get them to eat. We wanted to find a way to show this secretive behaviour, but we did not want to move into a naturalistic mode with realistic dialogue. Having just created two very physical movement sequences, we knew we had to find a different approach for this section.

Maxine recalled how uneasy she had felt during the opening sequence of the musical, *Cats*, when the cast came into the audience, stared at them at very close range and recited some of the poetry that the show was based on. Aisha also reminded us of a workshop we had taken part in, which dealt with personal space and the unpleasant feeling when someone is close behind you and you cannot see what they are doing. We liked the idea of audience confrontation, and experimented with the lower sixth group. We crouched in front of them very closely, and moved around them whispering words associated with secrets, such as:

You won't tell, will you?

It's a secret.

No one must know.

Can you be trusted?

You can't say anything.

We continued with the idea of working in an Artaudian manner, and this meant that we did not want to create any logical, realistic dialogue, or create a logical story line, but attack the audience with a series of images and sounds that would convey the horrors of anorexia. When we looked at the sequence, we were pleased with the impact it created. The lower sixth, who we had experimented with, also said that they felt very uncomfortable. Having created the right effect, we were not sure how to end the moment. After some discussion, we decided that the group members in the audience would fade their voices as they moved towards the exits (at each end of the cross).

Although the section with the raw meat was very powerful, we also wanted to show the reality of forced vomiting as it is a common part of the problem. Mia, who always looked for a visual impact, suggested that we should have one of the group actually vomit into a toilet bowl. We all thought the idea was gross, but after talking about it, we agreed that it would certainly shock the audience.

Colette suggested that we could juxtapose the ugliness against some glamorous fashion pictures and dreamy music to highlight the reality against the media image, but because of the performance layout that we had chosen, we could not project images. We still wanted the vomiting image however, and decided that we needed to represent this in some way. As we could not project anything, we decided that a real toilet pan would give the required sense of revulsion that we wanted, and so we bought a new white toilet pan, and then wondered how we could get it on stage. Colette suggested that we bring it on stage like a throne in a procession, and make the whole scene into a ritual. The school technicians mounted the pan on a piece of wood, and although it was very heavy, we managed to carry it on our shoulders and placed it in the centre of the cross.

We decided that, in order for all sectors of the audience to see one of the cast actually vomit, we would repeat the sequence with four of the cast while the rest moved amongst the audience repeating a well-known advertising slogan 'Because you're worth it', and giving the phrase a different inflexion each time. To create the actual vomit, each member who had to be sick chewed a custard cream biscuit with some milk, and held it in their mouth until they were over the bowl. It looked very realistic and several audience members groaned when it happened in front of them. When we watched the sequence on video, we were pleased with the impact and the irony of the ritual that we conveyed.

We needed to decide how to end the piece, but although we wanted to include some of the facts about the illness, we did not want to resort to any type of lecture. In the end, we decided to use sound and movement again. This time, we had 'Perfect' by Alanis Morissette playing, and gradually introduced the sound of a hospital heart monitor bleep, which got louder and louder until it drowned out the music. Whilst this was going on, we crossed the acting area wearing hospital-type dressing gowns, and as we passed the centre point, we dropped chocolate bars and food into a waste bin. Our movement got gradually slower as the beeping increased, and at the height of the volume, we used a **dead blackout (DBO)** together with an abrupt stop to the sound. At this point, there were no cast members on stage. After a long pause, we slowly brought up the house lights and played out the music. There was no **curtain call** or attempt to make any further contact with the audience. The sudden silence and images of 'lost' looking girls made the impact we wanted.

The finished work was very different from everything we had done up to that moment, and it was certainly very difficult to apply Artaud's ideas, but we were very satisfied with the finished product, and it was clear that our intended impact was created for the audience.

Key terms

dead blackout (DBO)
curtain call

Case study 6 (using an object as the stimulus)

Mohammed's group: Mohammed, Steve, Martin, Lucy, Alice, Aliya

Group background

We were a group of three girls and three boys in a sixth form college, each studying a range of A-level subjects. Apart from two of the girls, we had not worked together before we met to do the AS year of the Drama and Theatre Studies course. All the girls and one of the boys had some experience as we had done GCSE Drama.

During the first year of the course, for Unit 1, we studied *Ghosts* by Henrik Ibsen and *Oedipus Rex* by Sophocles and compared the idea of past events returning to affect the characters. We looked at the ideas of Stephen Berkoff, Bertolt Brecht, Edward Gordon Craig and Antonin Artaud. We also took part in two practical workshops led by visiting professional companies; one was on Brecht and the other was a *commedia dell'arte* session.

We saw many productions both in London and by small-scale touring groups at our local university theatre. One of the most enjoyable productions was *Noises Off* by Michael Frayn at the Royal National Theatre.

For Unit 2, we presented a wide range of monologues and duologues that showed the range of what we could do, and a performance of a shortened version of *Donkey's Years* by Michael Frayn.

Stage 1: Starting point

At the start of our Unit 3 project, we had a long discussion with our teacher about what we had to produce and what style of performance we wanted to work in. We agreed that we wanted to create comedy, as so many other A-level pieces we had seen were very serious and dealt with 'issues'. We all agreed that what we wanted to do was entertain a mixed audience of 16+ in a farcical manner. We had enjoyed working on the Michael Frayn play in the previous year and wanted to create something of our own in a similar style.

At the start of the next session, our teacher gave us a bell that you ring for attention in shops or hotels. We sat in a large circle and the teacher put the bell on an upturned **rostrum**. We then worked in pairs, one behind the desk and the other a customer with either a query, problem, complaint or other issue. We had to improvise the dialogue until we reached a satisfactory conclusion. The scenes we created were very comical and the exercise was great fun. The next stage was to begin an improvisation with the bell, and then others in the group joining at various intervals – all with different concerns.

> **Key term**
>
> rostrum

We decided from all the different situations we had developed, that some of the funniest were those set in a hotel. We agreed that we could develop several overlapping storylines in a typical tradition of farce. After reaching this decision, the next stage was to research the style of 'farce' and watch as many hotel sitcoms as possible.

Stage 2: Confirming the focus

At the next session, Steve brought in a box set of DVDs of *Fawlty Towers* and we spent some of the lesson watching these. We also talked about *Hotel Babylon* that was on TV, and some of the complicated plot lines that it had in it. Mr Alliston brought in several copies of *Hotel Paradiso* by Georges Feydeau and we took these away to read for the next session; we also had a look at *The Government Inspector* by Gogol.

When we next met, Mr Alliston asked us to write on a large sheet of paper all the elements of farce that we could identify. The result is shown below.

Very fast pace   Importance of timing   Larger than life characters

Lots of doors for rapid entrances and exits   Mistaken identity

Policemen   Vicars   A dead body   Depression

People in underwear/cross-dressing   Double entendre   Slapstick

Foreigners who cannot understand the language   Lost items/people

From research into the genre of farce, we discovered that they usually employed stereotypical characters. We knew about these from the *commedia* workshop and the notes that accompanied it.

Research notes

Another type of character is the stereotype or stock character, a character who reappears in various forms in many plays. Comedy is particularly a fruitful source of such figures, including the *miles gloriosus* or boastful soldier (a man who claims great valour, but proves to be a coward when tested), the irascible old man (the source of elements in the character of Polonius), the witty servant, the coquette, the prude, the fop, and others.

The *commedia dell'arte*, a popular form of the late Middle Ages and early Renaissance, employed actors who had standard lines of business and improvised the particular action in terms of their established characters and a sketchy outline of a plot. Frequently, Pantalone, an older man, generally a physician, was married to a young woman named Columbine. Her lover, Harlequin, was not only younger and more handsome than her husband, but also more vigorous sexually. Pantalone's servants, Brighella, Truffaldino, and others, were employed in frustrating or assisting either the lovers in their meetings or the husband in discovering them.

We decided that we would try to construct a basic plot line using as many of the elements of farce as we could, and then improvise around the story, filming our work and creating the script as we worked. Based on the idea of stereotypes and the notes above, we decided that the first step was to select characters that could operate within a storyline based on a hotel.

After a lot of discussion, we decided upon the following:

- The hotel manager – new, trying to impress and under pressure to succeed. (M)

- A lawyer visiting a client in prison. (F)

- A bird watcher who is searching for a rare bird. (M)

- A husband and wife celebrating their anniversary – but arguing all the time. (M and F)

- A ghost hunter who has got the wrong hotel. (F)

We spent some time talking about the possible moments of confusion that could come from some of these combinations, and realised that we needed to agree a time frame for the events, and also some incident that could act as a catalyst for all the characters.

As we did not want to sit and write a play, we decided that the events should take place over one day and night, and end the following morning. We then began an extended improvisation in which we began to try out our characters and introduce any elements that we thought might be interesting (in the style of circle improvisation that we were used to).

The characters gradually arrived at the hotel, were checked in and went to their rooms. Immediately we started to find problems:

- The bird watcher's room was no good because he had to have a view of the marshes.

- The husband and wife disagreed – he liked the room, but she did not (it did not have any atmosphere) – and this started them arguing.

- The lawyer was on her mobile phone to her client and was talking about the stolen jewellery that had never been recovered, and went into the wrong room.

- The manager was trying to calm down the couple and deal with the birdwatcher when the ghost hunter arrived and started listening to the walls with a stethoscope. The lawyer came out of the wrong room in time to see the ghost hunter listening to the wall of the room and thought that she was eavesdropping.

- The lawyer cut off her call, and went to the room that appeared to be number six, but the number nine had dropped and looked like six, so again she was in the wrong room – this time the bird watcher's new room.

All these events happened within the first ten minutes of improvisation and were a complete jumble. We had the ideas, but then had to explain to the rest of the group where we were and why. It was very clear that we could generate enough ideas to make the piece work, but it was also obvious that we would need to record ideas as we went along and then decide on a clear structure.

We carried on improvising in this manner and developing our characters and the relationships between them. The bird watcher was very secretive because he wanted a 'scoop' for spotting a very rare breed. The husband and wife decided not to speak to each other and only communicated through third parties. The ghost hunter just got weirder and would suddenly freeze and ask others if they could 'sense a presence'. The manager got more and more stressed as things went wrong and the lawyer got very suspicious. She was also very wary of the bird watcher as he was behaving so secretively. The ghost hunter wanted to get into the bird watcher's room, but he would not allow this as he thought that he was being spied on.

We also spent a session thinking of phrases that the characters might use quite innocently, but that would be misinterpreted by other characters. For example, the ghost hunter would say, 'I'm watching and listening: I'll find out what's what!' which sent the manager into a panic. The bird watcher said 'You wait! When I spot it, I'll be famous,' which made the lawyer suspicious. The husband and wife kept getting their argument tied up with other people's conversations as they would not talk to each other. This session was very helpful and we made notes of lots of possible phrases.

After several sessions trying out different scenarios, we thought it was time to create a secure structure together with a script so that we could begin work on the most important elements of blocking and movement, pace and timing, together with believable but 'larger than life' characters. We knew that, to make this type of play work, we had to generate a very fast pace and get the entrances and exits timed precisely with the dialogue. We also needed to create a set that had enough doors to make the situations plausible.

The discussion about the set almost stopped the production because we could not see any way to make the type of set we thought we needed. Mr Alliston came to the rescue again as he had arranged our next theatre trip which was to see *The 39 Steps*. Before we went, we had no idea what the play was about, except that it would be performed by four actors playing many characters. In order to get an idea of the content of the play, Mr Alliston brought in the film and explained that the theatre company had created a **pastiche** of the style. Having watched the film, we could not imagine how they could create the range of locations that it needed on stage.

Key term

pastiche

The performance was fantastic; some of the acting was in the style that we wanted to achieve, and seeing the actors really helped us to understand the idea of 'parody' that we had to create. More importantly, the way in which the actors used the stage and a variety of 'stage props' made us realise that we could do the same with our play. In *The 39 Steps*, there was a door on wheels that was constantly moved around the stage, and according to how it was used, it became either a crofter's cottage or the entrance to the library in the grand hall.

We were inspired by the production and decided that to create our hotel we would simply construct five, free-standing doors in frames and a counter for the reception. The rooms would be shown by the use of lighting for each space. Like *The 39 Steps*, we decided that we would have minimal furniture to leave maximum acting space. We approached the Design and Technology technicians to see if they could help with the construction of the doors, and were very fortunate as one of them was very interested in stagecraft and offered his services. During the next week, we all stayed after lessons and worked with Bill to make the doors. Mr Alliston funded the construction from the drama budget, as he said free-standing doors could be used on lots of different occasions.

Having solved one of the main problems and been enthused by the play we had seen, we spent the next few sessions writing our script.

Stage 3: Scripting the work

Although our original intention was not to spend time writing a script, we realised that in order to achieve the level of polish required for the genre, we would need to use our filmed ideas and experimental work and create a secure script.

This was a collective task and we all took turns to write down the dialogue and stage directions as they were suggested. We had done so much spontaneous improvisation earlier that many of the situations that we had developed were strung together to form a logical, if very farcical, sequence. The biggest problem with this task was that it was very time-consuming, and because we were developing the plot in a linear manner, we simply kept adding situations without looking ahead to a resolution. However, as a few of us had some free time in college, we offered to complete the script and bring it to the next session so that everyone could make suggestions and/or objections.

Stage 4: Polishing the work

The hardest part of the project was running the play over and over to make sure that we maintained the pace, and got our entrances and dialogue timed just right to create the humour we wanted.

After three weeks of polishing, we showed the finished play to the lower sixth during a general studies lesson; the teacher was going to use the play to discuss the idea of parody and how it is used in political writing and cartoons. We were very nervous because many of the students in the audience were not involved in drama or theatre and could be very critical. We presented the piece in the studio space as if it were the real performance. The run was fantastic with only a few minor mistakes that the audience didn't appear to notice.

Feedback from the group was excellent, but we were a little thrown by the amount of laughter and realised that we had not accounted for this in rehearsal. Mr Alliston explained about timing the dialogue to ensure that the audience's responses did not drown the next part of the dialogue. He also explained that, if the dialogue continues just as the laughter begins to fade, this will build the comedy over the next few lines to a crescendo.

Key term

corpsing (corpse)

We had a further week to iron out a few technical problems and improve the costumes and props that we wanted to use. Everyone raided the local charity shops to get costumes that were appropriate but 'exaggerated', and when members of the group came in with some outrageous clothes, we had to run the piece again a few times to prevent us '**corpsing**' whilst in character.

Martin, who was playing the bird watcher, had managed to get some thigh-length waders and a ludicrous hat with ear flaps; he also had a pair of huge binoculars and about six cameras hanging round his neck.

Mohammed, as the hotel manager, had acquired a tailed coat from a local amateur drama group, made a droopy, waxed moustache, and greased his hair and parted it down the centre.

Lucy, as the ghost hunter, wore a long loose-fitting paisley dress with a flowing shawl and very ornate dangly earrings – she looked like a fairground fortune-teller!

Alice, as the lawyer, wore a very businesslike black suit that was so tight she could hardly walk in it, and carried a black briefcase.

Aliya and Steve as the husband and wife decided to contrast their characters. Steve was wearing a tartan tank top with a bright yellow kipper tie and corduroy trousers, and Aliya was dressed as a classic 'bimbo' with very tight skirt and revealing 'boob tube'.

It was a very valuable exercise to rehearse the piece a few times in costume, as some of the movement we had planned was difficult and we had to get used to the changes; it was also important to get past the natural reaction to laugh at our fellow actors.

The last task was to select an appropriate piece of music to start and end the play. We all spent the next couple of days trawling through college archives and eventually agreed on the 'Liberty Bell March' by John Philip Sousa; as the theme tune to Monty Python's Flying Circus, we felt that everyone would immediately understand the comic nature of the play.

We all felt that the finished piece was very successful in achieving our objective, which was simply to entertain the audience members by showing them the antics and weaknesses of a bizarre group of individuals, all pursuing their own plans with no regard for anyone else. They enjoyed the spectacle, and the pleasure in performing was as great for the cast. A good time had by all!

REMEMBER: The case studies detailed above are only examples of some of the possible approaches, and you must not view them as recommendations for how you should approach the task.

SUPPORTING WRITTEN EVIDENCE

This Unit is *not* about creating a file of facts about the content of your performance, but rather a polished piece of theatre with an accompanying record of how it was developed.

For Unit 1 of your AS course, you will have submitted a set of Exploration Notes to a maximum of 3,000 words. There is no specified word count for your Supporting Written Evidence document for this unit, but you should allow about 2,000 words to record and evaluate the research and exploration process, and another 1,500 to evaluate the creative process and the final performance. Above all, you should aim to make your Supporting Written Evidence totally relevant and focused.

Your Supporting Written Evidence document must address the following *two aspects* of your work:

- the *research* that you undertake and how it was explored practically
- your evaluation of the *process* and final *performance*.

Keeping an ongoing record of your involvement in the creative process is very useful. Many actors keep a log of the work they do in preparation for performance, and in scripted productions the **assistant director** or stage manager will keep the prompt copy up-to-date at every rehearsal. This copy of the script shows all the essential moves and stage positions, as well as the technical cues for light, sound or set changes.

> **Key term**
>
> assistant director

You *do not* need to create a prompt copy, but some of the detail that this would contain should be in your Supporting Written Evidence document. Most importantly, you must provide details of the practical exploration of the work; in all the case studies, students described specific issues and how they resolved them to make sure the work conveyed their message or impacted on the audience in the desired manner.

Research

When you decide upon a topic, you will need to research and explore (practically) the content as thoroughly as possible. Remember this is 25 per cent of the Unit 3 marks.

> **Tip**
>
> Make sure that research does not become more important than practical development.

The research you undertake should not be a lot of theoretical detail from texts or the internet, but a mixture of knowledge about the topic and a clear understanding of how you explored both the content and theatrical form. It is important to remember that research is not only involved at the start of the project: you may need to find out about techniques during the development, or production possibilities towards the end of the process.

For example, the candidates in Case study 1 had to examine the issue they were addressing and re-examine their earlier practical work to decide which theatrical conventions would be appropriate. The students in Case study 2 needed to research the issue of immigration and the occupations of the characters they were creating to make the dialogue sound realistic. In Case study 5, the students needed to understand the facts about anorexia, so that they could structure their work around the realities of the illness, and they also had to explore the ideas of Artaud. In Case study 6, the group had to research the theatrical style of farce that they wanted to employ, to ensure that the essential components were included.

If the starting point for your work is based on a theme or issue, then you will need to find out about the topic. Any material from the internet must be filtered and interpreted, and not simply downloaded. Primary sources are usually more valuable than material found online; for example, talking to an immigrant about their experiences is often more useful than reading about statistics or government legislation. If you wanted to create a performance about the issues surrounding advertising, then the best source of information would be a person who creates advertisements.

If your starting point is an existing play, then you will need to read it carefully together with any commentaries on it. If possible, go and see a production of the play to see how others have interpreted it. When you are familiar with the play, you will need to discuss within your group the *aspects* you wish to focus on, the particular *meanings* you want to convey, or the *style* of performance you want to use.

The case studies show the type of information that you need to consider. You will see that many of the decisions made by the different groups were influenced by productions they went to see, or the practical work they did during their course or in workshops. You are expected to use your experiences as a performer and theatre-goer in the creation of work for this unit, and these will often form part of your research, or provide performance or production ideas to incorporate in your own work.

The table below shows the criteria that your teacher will use to mark your Supporting Written Evidence document for research and exploration for the piece. Key words and phrases have been underlined to remind you of the focus for your supporting evidence.

Assessment criteria	Level of response	Mark range
AO1 Research and exploration	Students demonstrate <u>outstanding depth</u> of research that is <u>far-reaching</u> and <u>comprehensive</u>. It is clear how the research has <u>directly influenced performance outcomes and practice</u> for both self and others.	13–15
	Students demonstrate an <u>excellent depth</u> of research that has produced a <u>significant range of influence</u> on performance outcomes and practice for self and others.	10–12
	Students demonstrate a <u>good depth</u> of research that has produced a <u>small range of influence</u> on performance outcomes and practice for self and others.	7–9
	Students demonstrate an <u>adequate depth</u> of research that has had <u>some impact</u> on performance outcomes and practice for self.	4–6
	Students demonstrate a <u>limited range</u> of research that shows <u>superficial understanding of the material and purpose of their enquiry</u>. Research activity has had <u>no impact</u> on performance outcomes or practice.	0–3

You need to show how the initial material has been researched and used to shape the work at significant stages in the process.

Some areas that could feature in your research and exploration are:

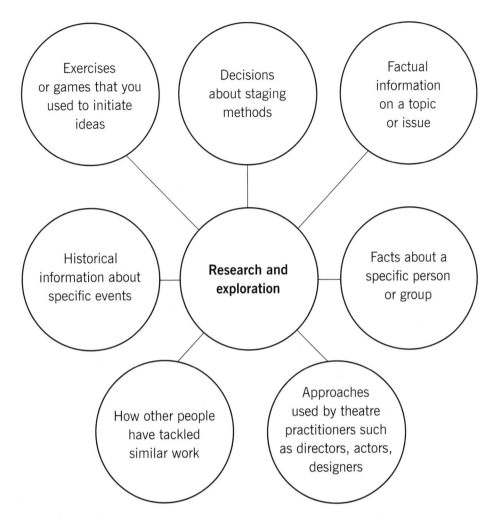

Development and structure

This section of your work will be assessed by your teacher(s) through continual monitoring of your involvement throughout the creative process. However, keeping a record of your practical involvement in the development of the work is very useful, as it will not only keep you on track to ensure that your initial ideas and objectives work on stage for an audience, but will also enable you to write your evaluation of the process and your intentions against the final outcome.

You should ask yourself some key questions:

- How did you create and extend your role(s) within the piece?

- What performance styles did your group explore, and how was the shape of the piece decided?

- What influence did recognised practitioners or live theatre productions have on the structure or style of your work?

- What were your initial intentions for the audience, and what impact or effect did you hope to achieve?

- What were the main problems that you encountered?

The headings below will guide you in the creation of your Supporting Written Evidence document. Drawings and diagrams can also be useful.

Aspect	Key points
Stimulus	Explain how the ideas for the work *evolved* from the starting point. Do not write about what you *did not* work on.
Decisions	Explain what your *intentions* were for the performance. Define who the work was meant for (*target audience*). Discuss how you intended to *engage* the audience.
Research	What did you need to find out about the *subject matter* of the piece? What research and/or practical exploration did you carry out on the *performance style(s)* that you used? What other *information* did you need to make your characters credible?
To help with the development of the work and your evaluation record:	
Key challenges	Focus on a few of the *theatrical moments* or *performance skills* that required a lot of input. Make sure you talk about *practical exploration* and the *application* of your research.
Practical detail	Depending on the style of the work, you could address some of the following as appropriate: • styles/genres used • use of the performance space – levels, depth and height • patterns of movement • pace of the production – how it was controlled • visual elements – set , costume, masks, make-up, etc. • creating specific moments of tension, humour, intrigue, irony • characterisation/roles • vocal demands • directing the audience focus • use of theatrical conventions • technical elements – recorded sound, lighting, special effects • influence of theatrical practitioners' ideas.
Assessing your progress	Discuss how your group *tested* the work to make sure it was fit for purpose. Show clearly how you responded to *feedback*, and detail aspects of the *refining* process.
Polishing	Explain how you *polished* the work to ensure it was totally *assured*.
Evaluation should consider	Actual against intended *impact* upon the audience. Objective assessment of *own and others'* level of *focus* and application of *skills*. What were your initial intentions for the audience, and how effectively were they communicated? Was the audience engaged? Focus on some specific moments or elements of the performance and clarify how and why they were effective.

Evaluation

The evaluation is part of the Supporting Written Evidence document, and you must make sure that you assess your involvement throughout the development process.

Your evaluation counts for 25 per cent of the marks for this unit and it must discuss the *process* as well as the final *performance*. If you have maintained a log of your involvement, the assessment of the progress of the work will be made easier. You must consider how successfully the final production managed to achieve the group's initial intentions. You must think about how your research influenced the work, and the practical methods by which you explored and agreed upon content or performance styles and conventions.

The evaluation is a personal document and requires you to take an objective and honest look at how you involved yourself in the process, and to what extent you achieved your objectives within your own performance. You must also consider how others in the group interacted with you and how their involvement and interaction with you affected your work.

The common failing with evaluations of performance work is that they become very descriptive and simply explain what the finished product was and how it was received by the audience.

Do not rely on audience questionnaires to provide your evaluation details.

Focus on a few key decisions and moments within the process that were important, and try to assess how you dealt with them in relation to others in the group. Similarly, determine how effective specific aspects of your performance were in the final production. Perhaps you wanted to change the pace of a series of lines to make the audience laugh, keep them in suspense or shock them. Was this achieved? Were there any special skills that you had to acquire for the piece? Were there particular moments that concerned you in rehearsal?

The table below shows the criteria that your teacher will use to mark your evaluation of process and final performance, which is part of your Supporting Written Evidence document. Key words and phrases have been underlined to remind you of the focus for your evaluation.

Assessment criteria	Level of response	Mark range
AO4 Evaluation	Students produce an <u>outstanding evaluation</u> of the <u>process and performance</u>. <u>Perceptive links</u> are made <u>between</u> the influence of <u>research, developmental activity and the performance</u> taking significant note of the <u>involvement of self and appreciative contribution of others</u>.	13–15
	Students produce an <u>excellent evaluation</u> of the <u>process and performance</u>. <u>Clear links</u> are made <u>between</u> the influence of <u>research, developmental activity and the performance</u> taking significant note of both the <u>involvement of self and others</u>.	10–12
	Students produce a <u>good evaluation</u> of the <u>process and performance</u>. They make a <u>range of links between</u> the influence of <u>research, developmental activity and the performance</u> taking full note of both the <u>involvement of self and others</u>.	7–9
	Students produce an <u>adequate evaluation</u> of the <u>process and performance</u>. <u>Some links</u> are made <u>between</u> the influence of <u>research, developmental activity and the performance</u> taking note of the <u>involvement of self but only superficial reference to others</u>.	4–6
	Students produce <u>limited evaluation</u> of the <u>process and performance</u>. <u>Few links</u> are made between the influence of <u>research, developmental activity and the performance</u> taking some note of the <u>involvement of self but no account of the contribution of others</u>.	0–3

The comments by candidates throughout the case studies reveal a range of approaches to the creative process, and the ways in which you can document and evaluate the research and development of the process and the final performance.

Below are two extracts from evaluations of the final performance. The first is very simplistic and describes personal issues and feelings that are not supported by reference to theatrical techniques, or focused on the actual performance. The second discusses the same aspects, but in a more focused and relevant manner using accepted theatrical terminology.

Here is a sample from a very subjective evaluation:

> On the night of the performance, everyone was really nervous and uptight, because one of the cast was very late arriving and we thought that they might not turn up. Everyone started to phone Jane to find out where she was, but her mobile was turned off and this made everyone worry even more. She arrived at the last minute and explained that her mum's car had broken down on the way and they had to get her dad to pick them up. (*This is all personal and says nothing about the performance*.) We just had time for a group hug before we had to start. (*The candidate could make a relevant point here about the lack of a proper warm-up for the performers*.)
>
> In the end, the play went <u>really well</u> and everyone in the audience enjoyed it and thought it was <u>great</u>. We wanted the play to amuse the audience and this we clearly did as they laughed at all the right moments. (*This has some relevance as it refers to the piece achieving its aims, but it needs more detail*.) No one forgot their lines or what they were supposed to do, and there were no problems apart from the fact that Andrea's coat had been left in the wrong place and so she could not change when she was supposed to enter from outside. (*Again this is about backstage procedures relating to props tables, but it is not fully developed*.) This looked a bit odd, but nobody seemed to notice.
>
> The lighting was <u>great</u> because Matt who operates the **desk** always does this job and really knows what is needed. (*There is no detail at all about the effectiveness of the lighting: intensity, speed, colour, direction, timing*.) Paul was doing the sound and this was a bit too loud at times. Some of the audience members said they could not always hear the speaking because of the music. (*This is about levels of volume, but gives limited detail*.)
>
> As I had found it difficult in rehearsals to remember my lines I was very worried that I would forget during the performance but I managed to remember everything. Another problem was not laughing in the scene with Tony about the broken vase but in the performance I managed to keep a straight face and deliver the lines seriously. (*Candidate could make valid observations about maintaining levels of concentration by referring to performance techniques*.) Our nerves made us all speak a bit faster and I think this was <u>better</u>.

Key term

desk

The evaluation is very subjective; in other words, it reflects the *feelings* of the writer, but does not give any *justified reasons* why she feels the way she does. The comments in brackets explain areas that could have been developed. Underlined words convey very little and require detailed explanations using accepted theatrical terms.

Here is an example of a more objective evaluation that addresses the same points in much more detail:

On the night of the performance, everyone was really nervous, and we had planned to carry out a full physical and vocal warm-up to ensure that our bodies and vocal cords would be flexible and appropriately relaxed to perform. Unfortunately, one of the cast was rather late and so the rest of us had to do this without her. We tried to make sure that her problems in getting to the venue did not add to the tensions of performing, and managed to involve her in the last part of the warm-up to prepare her for performing. (*The focus this time is on the preparation of the actors.*)

The performance was as we had planned in terms of the acting, and it appeared that our intention to amuse the audience had been successful as they laughed at all the right moments. (*This now acts as an overview of the success of the performance.*) Our levels of concentration were effectively sustained, and all the rehearsed moves and lines were delivered as planned. The success of the play depended upon maintaining our characters and timing the delivery of the dialogue and action to create the comic effect that was essential. Since our characters were larger than life, we did not have to engage in any great depth of emotion, but it was necessary to maintain the credibility of our characters and I was very conscious that I should not repeat problems with corpsing that had happened in rehearsal. (*The candidate has provided some specific details about aspects of the acting and performance that were effective and used theatrical terminology to express her views.*)

There were a few problems with the backstage organisation as Andrea's coat had been left in the wrong place and so she could not change when she was supposed to enter from outside. This looked a bit odd, but apparently nobody in the audience noticed and Andrea did not draw attention to it. In future we will need to ensure that we are more disciplined in setting out our props and making sure that we do not move any other actor's as we do not have anyone managing the props table. (*The problem is depersonalised and a potential solution suggested.*)

The lighting was very effective because Matt who operates the desk had worked with us during the development of the work and we had agreed all the lighting states at the technical rehearsals. The colours that we had agreed really helped to establish locations and time of day and all the changes were smooth and timed correctly, which added to the atmosphere that we were trying to create. (*Specific detail about why the lighting was effective.*) Feedback from the audience suggested that the musical underscoring, during the rapid question and answer section, was too loud and prevented them from focusing on the dialogue. I was not aware of this problem during the performance as the levels had been agreed during the technical rehearsal. In future we need to get a wider range of opinions on sound levels during the technical runs to make sure that they are suited to a wide audience profile. (*Detail of why the music was not as effective and a potential solution suggested.*)

The running time of the play was reduced by about five minutes and since nothing was cut, I assume that our delivery had been faster because of nervous tension; however, since the comedy depended on maintaining an effective pace in the delivery, this aspect actually enhanced the impact of the work. (*Sound reasoning offered for the increased pace and its impact on the work.*)

Tip

Remember: you must keep a record of your involvement in all aspects of the practical work from the very beginning. It is not good practice to create your Supporting Written Evidence document after you have finished the work.

These extracts only deal with aspects of the performance and clearly are much too short. In Unit 3, you must document and evaluate the *process* as well as the final *performance*. The case studies suggest a range of possible approaches to the task of documenting the process; some are more personal and descriptive than others, but all of them offer insights into how you could structure your account of the creative process.

Unit 4: Theatre Text in Context

What you need to know

- It is worth 60% of your A2 mark (30% of the total A level marks).
- It is divided into three sections, A, B and C. The marks are distributed 25% to Section A and 37.5% to each of Sections B and C.
- It is externally assessed through a 2 hour and 30 minute written exam paper.

What you have to do

You will extend your knowledge, understanding and skills of drama and theatre that you have gained through earlier units by studying *two plays* which were written and first performed before 1914. You will examine one play from the point of view of a theatre director, and analyse a live performance of your second play and consider its original performance conditions.

- In *Sections A and B* you are required to study *one* of the following plays:
  1. *Lysistrata* by Aristophanes (c. 411BC)
  2. *Doctor Faustus* by Christopher Marlowe (c. 1594)
  3. *Woyzeck* by Georg Büchner (1837).

Your teacher will advise you as to which one you will be studying at your centre and provide you with the approved version of the text. You will explore the selected play through workshops and, in the role of a director, develop ideas for your own production of it.

- In *Section C* you are required to see *a live performance* of a play and to study and research its original performance conditions.

You will consider how a director and his/her creative team and performers have interpreted the chosen play in a contemporary performance, and relate this experience to your understanding of the original performance conditions.

The play you see for Section C must be from a different period to the play you are studying for Sections A and B, and will be chosen by your teacher. The three given periods of theatrical development are:

- 525BC–AD65
- 1564–1720
- 1828–1914.

Although the assessment of Unit 4 is through a written exam, much of the preparation will be in the form of practical work. The work in this unit will build on the work you did for Unit 1 where you were required to study and work on two plays in detail, exploring them through practical activities and writing up your findings in a set of Exploration Notes.

Assessment objectives

This unit contributes to the assessment of objective 2 (10%), objective 3 (15%) and objective 4 (2.5%). Objective 2 assesses your knowledge and understanding of practical and theoretical aspects of drama and theatre, and your use of appropriate terminology; objective 3 assesses your ability to interpret a play, and objective 4 assesses your critical and evaluative judgement of live theatre. (See assessment grid on page 70.)

Examiner's tip

Ensure that you use the Edexcel prescribed play text throughout the course. Other copies of the play text can vary.

How you are assessed

Unit 4 is assessed by a written exam lasting 2 hours and 30 minutes. You can take your annotated copy of the script and your research notes into the exam with you to support you in answering the questions.

Section	Assessment requirements	Percentage of Unit 4 marks allocated
Section A	**Three** short questions based on an extract from your chosen set play (20 marks)	25%
Section B	**One** essay question from a choice of two about the set text (30 marks)	37.5%
Section C	**One** essay question from a choice of two about a live performance related to the original performance conditions (30 marks)	37.5%

SECTIONS A AND B

In this part of the course you will consider the play from the point of view of a director. You will learn about what directors do to prepare a text for production, how they handle rehearsals positively, and how they bring to life an interpretation of the play. You will be able to build on your experiences and the knowledge you gained when studying for the AS qualification.

In the exam, Sections A and B examine one set text from a choice of three. Section A provides you with an extract and asks you to think about it in rehearsal; Section B asks you to think about the play as a whole in production.

You are allowed to take an annotated copy of the text into the exam room to refer to when answering the questions.

This section examines each of the three plays in detail and gives some general advice on how to prepare for the written exam.

Working towards the exam

Your work at AS Level will have given you a good foundation to build on. You will have learnt a good deal about what it means to be an actor, director and (possibly) designer. The focus for this part of the course is on thinking like a director, but directors have to understand how actors and designers work and what they do. It will be useful to refer back to your AS work and to the AS Student Book from time to time.

A director's job is complex; it involves many skills and a good deal of knowledge. You have to work with a text, a group of actors, a group of designers and technicians – and, eventually, an audience. Firstly, you must make sure you understand the text – the words, the ideas, the social, cultural and historical background to it – and then you will develop ideas of your own about how you can bring it to life on stage in the 21st century. You need to know how to get a group of people to share your ideas, and then find the right techniques for rehearsal to help them make it work on stage for an audience. Here is the sequence of what you will do:

STUDY THE TEXT → DEVELOP IDEAS → REHEARSAL → PERFORMANCE

When you're working with your group during the year, you may find that these stages overlap or recur. You'll be doing a lot of developmental work, experimenting with ideas and techniques, so it won't be the same as just directing a play yourself. These stages do relate to the exam questions, though. Section A is about how you find the right rehearsal techniques to make your ideas work, and Section B is about explaining your ideas for a production of the play and how you will achieve them practically.

How to approach a set text

As a director, you have to be an expert on the text you are working with. You have to understand the text thoroughly and see it as drama, not literature. This means you have to translate your intellectual understanding of it into a way of making it work effectively on stage.

Preparatory work on the text

There are two areas you need to focus on:

1. Make sure you understand the language and the background. You need to read footnotes and introductions, for example. Your teacher will give you guidance about background research, and will help you to understand the social, cultural and historical context. You will then start developing your own ideas about the text.

2. Make sure you understand the dramatic potential of the text. Coming to grips with the characters and relationships is part of this, but you also need to see how the text is structured, both overall, and in smaller sections. You'll find ideas begin to flow as you look more closely at the text.

'Structure' is not always an easy idea to grasp, although it is obvious to everyone that plays (and sections of plays, such as scenes or acts) have a dramatic shape. You need to be aware of how CONFLICT builds into a CLIMAX and how a RESOLUTION then occurs. This pattern is often repeated at a lower level throughout the play.

Planning rehearsal activities

You need to choose and plan rehearsal activities. Your aim will be to find practical ways of helping the actors to share your ideas. Obviously, in a real situation you would listen to their ideas as well. In the exam situation, it's about *your* ideas, and how you put them into practice. For example, if it's an important part of your thinking about *Romeo and Juliet* that the two main characters should be seen as rather rich and spoilt at the beginning, then you might set up some improvisations with them bragging to their friends or behaving selfishly. (This is what Bertolt Brecht did when he wrote some practice scenes for *Romeo and Juliet*.)

Don't confuse 'warm-ups' with rehearsal techniques. Most rehearsals start with a physical and vocal warm-up, just like a football team getting themselves ready. As 'manager' you need to be thinking about the tactics, not just the warm-up. There are some standard rehearsal techniques which you'll have come across (for example: hot-seating, freeze-frames, role reversal, status exercises, improvisation), but directors often devise their own techniques to help their actors develop their roles. The important thing is to know what you want to achieve through the use of the technique.

Edexcel Examiner's tip

The examples you give of rehearsal techniques must be clear and purposeful. You need to be certain about *what* you want to achieve (and *why*), and *how* you intend to achieve it.

A note on improvisation

If you use this technique (and many directors do), you need to be clear about what you're trying to achieve. Think carefully about how you set the improvisation up, and what information and instructions you give to the actors. The more specific you are, the more successful the improvisation will be. During your AS course, you will have worked with the ideas of at least one recognised practitioner (an individual or a group). You may wish to adopt some of the rehearsal techniques which you have learnt about.

The role of the director

Your ideas about the play (the 'concept') will decide how you work with your production team and what you do in rehearsal. Having a 'concept' sounds rather grand and maybe daunting. You are free to be as adventurous and creative as you like, but don't feel that you must come up with an amazing new idea. Concepts don't have to involve moving time periods or setting the play in a rainforest; often ideas like this fail. You may simply have some positive ideas about a character or a relationship, or about the visual style of the production. Your ideas should arise out of the text, not be imposed on it; you will need to justify them.

Working with the production team

The most important members of the team for you are the stage manager (who holds the technical management of the production together), and the designers: the set designer (who will probably also design costumes and props), the lighting designer and the sound designer. They have to share your ideas and translate them into what the audience sees and hears. For the exam, you must be able to explain your ideas about the production (and the reasons) to the team (for example, if you want lighting to be 'cold' or 'warm', low-level or bright); you don't need to be a technician, but you do need to explain your production ideas clearly and how you think they can work.

Working with the actors

You will have planned your rehearsal activities (see page 71). Directors have to be flexible and sometimes change their tactics from day to day – but the important thing is to know what you intend to achieve in a rehearsal. Hold on to your ideas and plan positively. Don't forget the importance of voice and movement on stage (think back to your work on vocal awareness and non-verbal communication in your AS course).

Stagecraft

Edexcel Examiner's tip

Think about how you are going to annotate your text – too much annotation can be confusing – it has to be useful to you in exam conditions. Include reminders of your directorial ideas (your interpretation) and some rehearsal ideas for particular sections. Remember that you can use symbols (numbers or abbreviations, for example) to link sections.

How you get your actors to use the acting space is vital, so you need to consider elements like positioning on stage, distances between characters, the use of levels and the placing of important items of set.

Using specialist language

Make sure that you use appropriate specialist vocabulary when answering the questions: terms associated with Stanislavski's approach, such as objective, unit, obstacle, Emotion Memory, sub-text; Brecht's *Verfremdung* (translated as 'estrangement' or 'alientation') or Artaud's 'theatre of cruelty'; specific rehearsal techniques such as 'conscience alley' and 'spotlighting'; and terms associated with stage forms and the use of space, such as thrust, promenade, upstage, downstage, proxemics.

LYSISTRATA

Lysistrata is an Ancient Greek **comedy** in which the women of Athens campaign for peace by refusing to have sexual relations with their husbands until they stop the conflict with Sparta.

The play was written and first performed in 411BC at a time of extreme political upheaval and the events of the day provide the backdrop to the drama.

So what could a modern audience find appealing about a play written almost 2,500 years ago about some long-forgotten war? The simple answer is that the play has sex appeal, which directors, performers and audiences never seem to lose interest in. It also deals with the universal theme of war and the human race's inability to live in peace. Lysistrata's desperate wish to live in peace, and Aristophanes' portrayal of the ridiculousness of men who use violence to solve the world's problems, still resonate with us today.

Aristophanes' simple notion of creating a situation based on sexual frustration gives the play an integral element of dramatic tension and boundless comic potential. The framework of characters and circumstances that Aristophanes has created provides a wealth of theatrical potential waiting to be explored and interpreted by directors and performers.

The following pages will help you appreciate the significance of Aristophanes as a dramatist and the directorial opportunities to which *Lysistrata* lends itself. The background information on Aristophanes and on *Lysistrata* will help you understand the context of the play. You will find guidance on the decisions you, as a director, will need to make about your own interpretation of the play.

What do we know about Aristophanes?

Aristophanes was born around 448BC and died around 385BC. His plays are the only known examples of this oldest form of Greek comedy. Aristophanes came from a wealthy family, but became an apprentice to the theatre, establishing his reputation when his first known play, *Banqueters,* was produced in 427BC.

Aristophanes produced some 40 plays, of which only 11 have survived. He was at his most creative during the time of civil war between Athens and Sparta (431–404BC), and the politics and corruption surrounding this conflict serve as a background to *Lysistrata* and many of his other plays from this period.

Timeline

c. 448BC	Aristophanes, son of Philippus, was born in Cydathenaeum, a district in Athens.
430–428BC	Aristophanes collaborates with other writers, training to become a dramatist.
428–427BC	Aristophanes enters his play, *Banqueters* (lost), in the City Dionysia festival, winning second prize.
426BC	*Babylonians* (lost) wins first prize.
425BC	*The Archarnians,* his earliest surviving play, wins first prize.
424BC	Aristophanes writes and produces his first play (*The Knights*) for the festival of Lenaea, winning first prize.
423BC	Aristophanes receives a setback when his play *The Clouds* is unsuccessful.
422BC	*The Preview* (lost) and *The Wasps* win first and second prizes respectively.
421BC	*Peace* wins second prize.
419–418BC	Aristophanes makes revisions to *The Clouds*, but it is never produced. This version has survived.
414BC	*The Birds* wins second prize in the City Dionysia festival.
411BC	*Lysistrata* and *Thesmophoriazusae* (a play about a women's festival which parodies Euripides' work) are produced.
406BC	The death of fellow playwrights, Euripides and Sophocles.
405–404BC	*The Frogs*, in which the god Dionysus travels to the underworld to fetch Euripides back from the dead, wins first prize. Aristophanes is awarded public honours and *The Frogs* is restaged.
391–390BC	*Ecclesiazusae* (or *The Assemblywomen*) is produced and Aristophanes is elected to serve on Athens' governing body, the *Council of Five Hundred*. (see p77)
388–386BC	*Plutus* (or *Wealth*), Aristophanes' last surviving play, is produced, followed by *Cocalus* (387BC) and his last known play *Aolosicon* (386BC). The latter two were produced by his son, Araros.
c. 385BC	Aristophanes dies, leaving his two sons, Araros and Philippus, to follow in his footsteps as dramatists. Regrettably none of their plays have survived.

NB: These dates are approximate, as our knowledge of the period is quite fragmentary and it is virtually impossible to be precise, so there may be some variance with other sources.

The text of the play

Lysistrata is the oldest of the three plays you can study in Unit 4, but the text is the most modern because it is a 20th-century translation from the original Ancient Greek. The version of *Lysistrata* you are using for the exam is by Professor Alan H. Sommerstein of the University of Nottingham, which he published in 1973 and revised in 2003.

A performable English version of Aristophanes' original has to strike a careful balance between remaining relatively faithful to the playwright's actual words, but at the same time communicating effectively to a modern audience. The text you are using is not a word-for-word translation of the Ancient Greek, but neither is it an adaptation; it is close to Aristophanes' original in spirit and meaning, but the translator has taken the following approach:

'Passages of spoken verse are translated as prose, and passages of song are translated as verse; but one or two spoken passages in which the **diction** or **metre of tragedy** is imitated are rendered in **blank verse**, and the speeches in the **parabases** (which were probably declaimed in strict rhythm to musical accompaniment) in **rhymed verse**.' (Sommerstein, 2003, page iii)

Key terms

diction/metre of tragedy
tragedy
blank verse
parabasis (pl. parabases)
rhymed verse
personification

You should be aware that none of the stage directions in the Edexcel edition are in Aristophanes' original and that they are only there for guidance. Note also that the characters from Sparta have been given a Scottish accent to suggest that they are from a different part of the country. Any translation will take liberties with the text because it is necessarily a process of interpretation, and for this reason it gives you as a director a considerable amount of licence to play around with it to bring it to life on the stage.

Activity 1

Look at the section from Lampito's entrance on page 11 to the women's exit on page 33.

a) Experiment with giving the Athenians, Spartans (Boeotians) and Corinthians different regional accents and give reasons for your final choice.

b) Edit the text to fit the dialects and regional accents you have selected.

c) There are more characters on stage than have speaking lines in this scene. Experiment with redistributing the lines between more characters and creating additional 'response and reaction dialogue' for the non-speaking characters.

Synopsis

The city-states of Athens and Sparta have been at war with each other for around 20 years and Lysistrata has called together the women of Greece to force the men to stop fighting.

Lysistrata has two ideas to bring about peace: one is to persuade all Greek women to withhold sexual favours from their husbands, and the other is to seize the Acropolis, where all the money of the state is kept, so that the rulers will be unable to pay the army. The women eventually agree to the sex strike and they swear an oath together.

The old men of Athens attempt to recapture the Acropolis, but they soon retreat when the women pour water over them. A city magistrate attempts to reclaim the Acropolis, but he is humbled when the women dress him up in their feminine clothing and treat him like a corpse at a funeral.

Lysistrata expresses concern that many of her followers are beginning to weaken and slip away to see their husbands. She persuades them to continue with their sex strike. A young soldier, Cinesias (whose name means 'randy'), experiences growing sexual frustration as his wife, Myrrhine, teases him with the promise of sex, only to withdraw it when he refuses to agree to peace.

Finally, an ambassador from Sparta arrives to discuss terms for peace with the Athenians. The men are unable to agree, and Lysistrata uses the presence of a naked woman (the **personification** of Reconciliation) as a distraction to broker a peace treaty. The play ends in a celebration of song and dance.

Edexcel Examiner's tip

You must ensure that you have the prescribed text from Edexcel. This version has space for you to write notes and the examiner will be referring to the same version – if you use page numbers from a different version in the exam, the examiner will not know which lines you are referring to. Only the prescribed version will be permitted in the exam room.

Notes on the names

Lysistrata: pronounced liss-i-STRAH-ta. Means 'releaser of armies'.
Calonice (or Kalonike): pronounced cal-on-EE-kee. Means 'fine victory'.
Myrrhine: pronounced mi-REE-nee. Means 'myrtle wreath' or 'sexpot'.
Cinesias (or Kinesias): pronounced kin-e-SEE-ass. Means 'randy'.
Lampito: pronounced lam-pi-TOH. Means 'her Excellency'.
Manes: pronounced MAH-nees.
Stratyllis: pronounced strat-ILL-iss. Means 'General's wife'.

Key term

personification

Social, cultural and historical context

For both Section A and Section B of the exam, you will answer questions on the play from the point of view of a director. In order for you to be able to make any directorial decisions about the play, you need to have some insight into the background surrounding the play's original conception and performance. One of the attractions for you as a director of a modern production of *Lysistrata* is that its origins are so distant from us, and the social and cultural conditions are so different from ours, that it is possible to do almost anything with the play to enhance its contemporary relevance.

As a piece of theatre, *Lysistrata* has the potential to be extremely funny. However much the world may have changed in 2,500 years, one thing that has remained constant is that the sight of an actor adorning a large erect penis encourages as much laughter from an audience now as it did then. There is an almost 'anything goes' attitude amongst directors when it comes to *Lysistrata*, and very little reverence is paid to the text.

Activity 2

Using your knowledge and understanding of the social, cultural and historical contexts of the original, consider when and where your own interpretation of the play will take place.

a) What sort of parallels with the original will your version have?

b) In what ways will your version differ from the original and why?

Athens in the 5th century BC

At this time, Greece was made up of a number of autonomous city-states, each governing a small empire and competing with its rivals. In the early part of the century, the city-state of Athens had achieved wealth and success through the leading role it played in defeating the Persian invaders.

From 431 to 404BC, Athens was engaged in a fruitless conflict with the neighbouring city-state of Sparta and her allies. This was known as the Peloponnesian War, and the violence of the conflict is the context for Aristophanes' play. Athens was an imperial power under the leadership of Pericles, but it was also the most advanced democracy in the known world. Its wealth was evident in buildings such as the temples on the Acropolis and the theatre. Aristophanes lived at the same time as some of the most influential dramatists (Sophocles and Euripides) and philosophers (Plato and Socrates) in the civilised world.

Athens was not a particularly large city by modern standards; the city and its surrounding area, Attica, had a population of around 300,000, about half of whom lived in the city itself. Although it called itself a democracy, about half the population were slaves with no political rights, and some 25,000 people were considered to be foreigners and had no status as citizens. Women from all classes in society had no rights at all. In reality, only about 10–15 per cent of the male population could be said to be part of the democracy.

Taking it further

You will find more detailed background information on Athens and her rivalry with Sparta in the introduction to Sommerstein's edition (see page 86).

There was also a hierarchy of class based on wealth, and considerable favour was given to individuals of high birth and who were connected to good families. However, it was a close-knit society, one in which the entire community could attend mass meetings and witness the decision-making process at first hand. Each year five hundred citizens were selected to sit on what was known as the Council of Five Hundred. This was effectively the equivalent of our modern day parliament and it provided an opportunity for those selected to take part in debates and to influence the way that Athens was governed. However, the Council of Five Hundred was only democratic in the sense that an equal number of men of high birth or wealth were selected by those in high office from each of the ten tribes of Athens.

Religion

A belief in the divine and in the higher power of the gods was central to the Ancient Greek way of life. The gods provided the Greeks with an explanation of how the world was created, and gave them the reasons for the way things happened as they did. Ritual worship was an integral part of the daily routine for everyone, and the gods were to be treated with awe, fear and sometimes laughter, but the intention was always to please them, knowing that humans were mere playthings of a higher power.

The great temple built in honour of the goddess Athena dominated the city landscape. The theatre, situated to the southeast below the Acropolis, was dedicated to the god Dionysus: the theatre was holy ground and Dionysus was its god, and everything that went on in his theatre was performed to please him.

The gods

Zeus: the father of the gods, of humankind and the known universe.
Athena: daughter of Zeus and a warrior goddess, protector of civilised life in its many forms such as the arts and crafts and agriculture.
Dionysius: (also known as Bacchus) the god of wine, fertility and growth; his love of ritual and celebration meant that he was the perfect religious figure to be connected with drama and the theatre.
Aphrodite: goddess of beauty, love and sex.

Theatre of Dionysus as viewed from the Acropolis

According to Sommerstein, Lysistrata's scheme of wives withholding sex from their husbands could only have been believed by the mainly male audience of the day because she was supported by the gods:

'Aphrodite, the goddess of the sexual process, ensures that the men are quickly brought to the last stage of physical desperation, while the virgin Athena ... through her agent Lysistrata strengthens the women to endure abstention for the time necessary for the scheme to succeed.' (Sommerstein, 2003, page 136)

Performance history

The cultural life of Athens in the 5th century BC was built around a number of religious festivals, each dedicated to the worship of different gods. Drama was a central activity in Athenian society and the audience for a single performance was somewhere between 17,000 and 30,000 people. Performances took place in the open air during daylight hours.

There were two annual drama festivals in Athens: the Lenaea and the City Dionysia. The Lenaea was a more domestic affair, which is why the focus was on comedy and **satire**, and why it is believed that *Lysistrata* was premiered there. The festival was a competition where the plays to be performed were selected by the *Archon*, a magistrate, who also chose a *choregos* (plural *choregoi*) for each play. The role of choregos was a civic and prestigious duty for those who had wealth to sponsor and fund a play. A choregos would pay for the training of the **Chorus** and purchase the props, costumes and masks. The play would usually be produced by the playwright (or poet as they were called at the time) who might also play a leading role.

It is likely that Aristophanes worked with a choregos to produce *Lysistrata*, but there is no evidence to suggest that he was an actor.

In the audience, preference was given to the wealthy and those of high birth, who would take along their servants. It was the custom for women to stay at home to manage the household, so the only female presence at the first performance of *Lysistrata* is likely to have been servants.

On stage, there were no women either and all of the performers would have been men wearing masks, whichever gender they were portraying. It is likely that the situation portrayed in the play would have been perceived as highly preposterous. The majority of the male audience would have found it unbelievable and laughable that women in their society could take control of the treasury and the bedroom as Lysistrata and her followers do. In a modern context of equal rights between the sexes and, in some respects, the sexual supremacy of women over men, the situation can be seen quite differently.

Interest in *Lysistrata* as a performance text in English had to wait for nearly two thousand years after its first performance in 411BC. Early performances of Greek drama in England, and in particular that of Aristophanes, were confined to amateurs and to university student drama groups such as those at Oxford and Cambridge. The bawdiness of *Lysistrata* was far too outrageous for Victorian audiences, and any attempt at producing a version for the professional stage containing strong language or approximating the lewdness of the original, had to await the abolition of theatre censorship in Britain in 1968.

Form and structure, genre and style

The **form** of a play is to do with the way in which the playwright structures the content. **Genre** is a way of categorising a play and identifying it with other plays of a similar type. **Style** is the distinctive characteristics that a playwright brings to the way he or she uses form and genre and is further extended in the theatre by the means that are used to interpret a play in performance by a director, designers, actors and musicians.

Key terms

satire
Chorus

For more information about Greek theatre and staging conditions, see pages 124-133.

In 2006, a group of girlfriends and wives from the Colombian city of Pereira mounted a sex strike in protest against their partners and husbands who were involved in gang crime. The purpose of withdrawing conjugal rights was to speed up the process of disarmament and to lower the rate of violent crime in the country. By all accounts, this action was taken seriously and had some effect in reducing crime.

Key terms

form
genre
style

Form and structure

The form and structure of *Lysistrata* is partly determined by the rules that Aristophanes had to follow in writing his play for a festival competition. Aristophanes had only four (possibly five) leading actors and a Chorus at his disposal. The Chorus was made up of between 15 and 24 performers. The Chorus in *Lysistrata* is unusual because it is spit into two groups of men and women, although all of them would have been played by men. Within the rules of Ancient Greek tragedies and comedies, once the Chorus has entered, it has to remain, which creates certain restrictions. With the principal characters, there would have been considerable doubling and trebling of roles with the differentiation of characters achieved through a change of mask. Lampito, for example, is introduced at the beginning of the play, but never reappears after her exit into the Acropolis (page 33). There are several non-speaking roles which were probably given to slaves, as this would have kept production costs down.

There are no stage directions or scene divisions indicated in the original text, but the overall structure of the play follows this pattern:

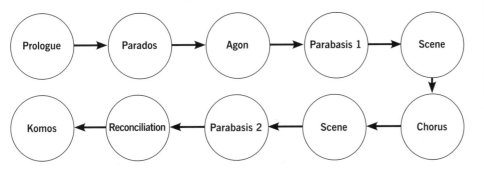

Key terms

prologue
parados
agon
komos

Prologue ↓	Scene between the women where Lysistrata sets out her plan. The women take the sacred oath to abstain from sex.
Parados ↓	Entrance of the Chorus of Old Men. The Old Men try to light a fire outside the Acropolis to smoke out Lysistrata and her companions. Entrance of the Chorus of Old Women. They manage to pour water over the men and their pyre.
Agon ↓	The angry magistrate confers with Lysistrata and attempts to regain control of the Acropolis. He loses the argument and loses his dignity when the women dress him up as a corpse.
Parabasis 1 ↓	The Chorus of Old Men attempt to take on the Chorus of Old Women and are temporarily defeated.
Scene ↓	Some of the women are weakening, and Lysistrata struggles to prevent three of the women from returning to their husbands.
Chorus	The Old Men and Old Women exchange tales and further insults with each other.
Scene ↓	Cinesias appears with his phallus fully erect and is teased mercilessly by his wife Myrrhine. The Old Men sympathise with Cinesias. A Spartan herald comes to announce that they want to make peace because, like the Athenians, the Spartan men are suffering from sexual frustration too.
Parabasis 2 ↓	Stratyllis, leader of the Chorus of Old Women, makes peace with the leader of the Chorus of Old Men and removes an insect from his eye. The Old Women and Old Men kiss and make up and become one united Chorus.
Reconciliation scene ↓	A delegation of Athenian and Spartan leaders, each with erect phallus, meet to negotiate peace. Lysistrata acts as arbitrator and leads both sides off to sign the treaty and the women entertain them.
Komos	After a short interlude from the Chorus, some drunken Athenians appear saying what a wonderful party they have had with the Spartans. They are joined by some drunken Spartans and their leader sings them a song. Lysistrata enters to return the Athenian and Spartan wives to their husbands. The play ends with songs and dances as a celebration to everlasting peace and joy.

Genre

Lysistrata belongs to a genre that has become known as Aristophanic Comedy, a subcategory of Old Comedy (associated with the 5th century BC) as opposed to the New Comedy of the 4th century BC. Old Comedy is generally about ridiculing the politics and individuals of the time, whereas New Comedy deals with character types and is an early form of comedy of manners. The word 'comedy' is linked to the Greek word 'komos', meaning a processional celebration, which may also have provided the origins of the theatrical genre we call comedy. Greek comedies often end with a section known as the komos, which is evident in *Lysistrata* with its celebratory conclusion of drunkenness, revelry, song and dance.

Style

As a director, you will inevitably bring your own stamp to bear on the way that you interpret the play and this will be your style of presentation. Style is concerned with the look and the feel of the production, and is largely determined by the director and the creative team of designers, composer and choreographer: the style of a production is about deciding how you want to stage it.

Phil Wilmott's production of Germaine Greer's version of *Lysistrata,* for example, is set in a bathhouse where the old generals lie around in towels and are serviced by a Chorus of older women. The style of acting required is that of a *Carry On* film and Wilmott cites *Carry On Cleo* as an example. The costumes consist of mainly towels and different colours are used to differentiate between the Spartans and the Athenians. The looseness of the towels means that they provide an effective visual device to graphically illustrate the level of sexual arousal amongst the male characters which is inherently funny. The choice of music is popular songs from the 1950s, which in itself also influences the style of the production.

Scene from Germaine Greer's version, set in a bath house

Rehearsal techniques

In the exam you will be asked to suggest exercises you would use in rehearsal to explore characters and their relationships. The following provides some examples of possible rehearsal techniques.

Activity 3 – Gestus

Using Brecht's idea of *gestus*, find the appropriate combination of facial expression, vocal intonation and body language to express the difference between characters in the play.

Organisation:

One actor is in the role of a television interviewer. Choose three or four different characters from the play (e.g. Lampito and the Magistrate) and play out an improvisation where the TV interviewer is asking for their views on the current Sex-strike and the women's capture of the Acropolis. Record the outcomes on DVD.

Analysis:

Watching the recording, isolate gestures and speech patterns and see how they differ depending upon the character's point of view. Incorporate these observations into the rehearsal process.

Activity 4 – Archetypes

In general terms, the characters in *Lysistrata* are two-dimensional or archetypes, and they represent ideas rather than genuine emotions. They have broad and obvious personality traits rather than subtle characteristics with psychological depth.

Here is a list of adjectives describing four of the play's characters, to which you can add your own.

Lysistrata	Magistrate	Calonice	Myrrhine
Independent	Officious	Aggressive	Sexy
Intelligent	Pompous	Agreeable	Alluring
Strong-minded	Affronted	Strong	Passionate

Organisation:

The adjectives are written out on separate pieces of paper, folded up and put into a hat or a bag. Each player in turn pulls out a piece of paper and has to find a way of acting out the word described on the piece of paper. The rest of the group observe the player's actions and have the opportunity to give feedback and make further suggestions.

Analysis:

Both the player acting out the word and the observers should note down how a particular stance, movement or gesture provides a strong visual image that suggests particular words. The point of this exercise is for the player to really exaggerate their movements to help them find a physical representation of their character trait.

Directing *Lysistrata*

As a director you have to make some important decisions about your approach to staging *Lysistrata* before you go into rehearsal. The design concept for the production and the framework for your exploratory work with actors in rehearsal will flow from your overriding idea for the play. You need to show your awareness of how all the production and performance elements outlined below come together under the guiding hands of a director to create a piece of theatre.

Activity 5 – The director's starting point

As a director, here are some of the initial questions you need to ask yourself. Recording your responses will help you on the way to formulating your own production concept for *Lysistrata.*

a) How much is my budget?

b) How will I cast it in terms of gender and the number of performers?

c) What sort of stage space will I be working in?

d) What is my 'take' on *Lysistrata:*

- Is it a peace or anti-war play?

- Is it a play about sexual equality or inequality?

- Is it a bawdy farce?

- Is it a political play?

- Is it an historical record of Greek life in the 5th century BC?

- Is it a satire?

- What is it really about for me?

e) How will I deal with the comedy?

f) How will I treat the Chorus?

g) When and where will I set it?

h) What sort of song and dance will I use?

i) Will I use masks and, if so, what type of masks?

The translator, Sommerstein, says of the scene on page 147: 'It is very difficult to be sure what is going on in this scene, or even what characters are involved in it. My identifications and stage directions are based on the assumption that the Athenians, being drunk, drive the Spartans' slaves away (as they will later do a second time) in the mistaken belief that they are doing their new-found friends a good turn.' As director, you might find a much improved solution to this problem.

Will you adapt the text?

Trying to be faithful to the text is not an option when it comes to directing your production of this particular play. You must use the Edexcel version as the starting point, but as you work on it, you may find that it needs cutting or altering to make it more performable.

All of the section transitions need particular attention, as it is not always clear how scene changes should occur. The transition between pages 146 and 147, for example, is odd because there is hardly enough time allowed for the Spartans and the Athenians to get drunk and sign the peace treaty.

How will you deal with the comedy?

The comedy in the play is both verbal and visual. The play is certainly funny, but you have to decide the extent to which you want to 'play it for laughs': there is a difference between actors saying and doing something that is knowingly funny to them and to the audience, and playing something for real which happens to come across as funny.

In comedy, timing is very important, and there is an art to placing the emphasis on the right word and waiting for the right moment to say a line in order to gain the greatest laugh. Some actors are natural comedians and this may influence the way that you cast some of the roles.

A script can only provide an indication of the opportunities for visual comedy and *Lysistrata* is bursting with them. For example, the first scene between the Old Men and Old Women (pages 43–51) will have the tone set by the way the actors move and how old and decrepit they appear.

Period or contemporary?

The choice is yours, but you need to think about how you are going to deal with the references to the Peloponnesian War and to Ancient Greek gods and myths. The play has no real basis in reality, so you can decide a time and place to suit your interpretation as long as you justify your decision.

How will you cast your production?

The number of performers you use, and the way they are deployed, will define the style of your production in terms of scale. If taken literally, the Edexcel version would require a cast of around 60, but with a reduction in the size of the Chorus and some multiple role-playing, it could be played with a cast of 15 to 20. You will need to map out your casting across the play.

What will your production look like?

This will be determined to some extent by where and when you decide to set the play and what kind of space you intend to use. Your approach to how the play looks will be part of your overall production concept. For example, if you opt for a physical theatre way of working, there may be very little scenery and the bodies of the actors can be used to create walls and doors. The original setting for the play suggests a large open space in front of the gates of the Acropolis, with the women looking down from the ramparts. This use of height and space can just as easily be created physically by the actors as it could by using some sort of designed physical structure. There is no need to take any notice of the stage directions in the script, so the opportunities for the setting of the play are completely open-ended.

Lysistrata lends itself just as much to a minimal use of scenic design as it does to something more expansive and complex. In many ways the costumes are more important to the look of the production than the setting, because they can indicate period, location and character status and age more effectively than a lavish set can. Using colour to differentiate between Athenians and Spartans is a simple device and acts as an instant visual identifier for the audience; taking the idea in the script that the Spartans speak Scottish could be followed through in the design by dressing them in tartan, for example.

Tip

The use of 'anachronism', when something is deliberately placed out of its time, is an accepted theatrical convention.

What will your production sound like?

There are two aspects to consider here: the accents the actors use and the use of music. In the Edexcel version, the Spartan characters use a Scottish accent to distinguish them from the Athenians. You might want to choose an appropriate accent to distinguish your character groups, and alter the dialogue accordingly. You might compose your own songs or use existing popular or folk songs to replace those in the text. You should consider how you might use sound effects to suggest time, place and action; for example, a news bulletin on the progress of the war might help to effectively transpose the action of the play to the 20th century.

The choice of music is important too. Just as bagpipes might suggest Scotland, the use of panpipes could suggest a South American setting, or the guitar a Spanish setting. We have no records of what Greek music of the period sounded like, but there is evidence to suggest that it was used to accompany spoken dialogue as well as being used in the form of songs.

Masks or no masks?

A feature of Greek drama is that all the actors wore masks. Originally these masks were made of wood with linen fabric stretched over them. The mouth section was built out at the front so that it would act as a loud-hailer to carry the actor's voice around the theatre. Each character's mask was different in design.

The decision to use masks in your production is fundamental as it will contribute to the overall style and approach. The masks should be carefully designed to provide you with the right kind of blank canvas that you want an actor to bring to life. Acting with masks is a particular skill and requires the actor to use exaggerated movement and to communicate more with the audience than with each other. The use of stylised make-up, as in the Japanese **Kabuki theatre**, is a useful compromise. If you want to make use of facial expressions, then you should consider not using masks at all.

Key term

Kabuki theatre

How will you handle the Chorus?

The Chorus is a key element in any play written during this period. Aristophanes' use of the Chorus in *Lysistrata* is unusual in that he has divided it in two to become the opposing forces of the Old Men and Old Women. You will need to make some decisions about your use of the Chorus:

- How many actors are you going to use?

- Will you be using masks?

- Will you have a uniform look or distinguishing features for each member of the Chorus?

- Will members of the Chorus be playing other parts?

- How will the Chorus move? Will they stand close together or be spaced out? Will they have individual movements or be choreographed in some way?

- How will the lines be spoken? Will you assign different lines to individual actors or will they be spoken in unison?

- Many of the Chorus sequences are song lyrics (e.g. pages 35–37, 41–43); how will you set them to music and how will you stage them?

Interpretation

For Aristophanes all those centuries ago, the idea of women wielding power through the use of sexual favours was as much a momentary theatrical dream as the bringing about of peace between his fellow Greeks in the warring states of Athens and Sparta.

The status of women and sexual politics might be quite different today in the Western world, but little has changed when it comes to the dominance of men in warfare. The subject matter of the play is as relevant as it was at its first performance, and the sight of a rising bulge in the crotch of a man's trousers is as potent a comic image as it ever was.

There have been countless productions of, and variations on, *Lysistrata* in the last century and a half, and the table below gives a few examples of some of the more interesting ones. They provide evidence of how the play lends itself to being given a new makeover each time it is approached and interpreted by a different production team.

Key terms

Opéra comique
libretto

1885	**Opéra comique** loosely based on *Lysistrata*, music by Eugène Feautrier, **libretto** by Etienne Lettry.
1892	French version by Maurice Donnay, produced by the Comédie Française at the Grand Théâtre, Paris. Gabrielle Réjane played Lysistrata.
1908	German version in a translation by Leo Greiner. Produced at the Deutsches Theater und Kammerspiele, Berlin. Directed by Max Reinhardt with music by Engelbert Humperdinck.
1910	Earliest recorded British professional production of *Lysistrata* in a version by Laurence Housman. It starred Gertrude Kingston and was performed at the Adelphi Theatre by the Little Theatre Company.
1923	Russian production at the Moscow Art Theatre, directed by Stanislavski's partner, Vladimir Ivanovitch Nemirovitch-Dantchenko. The production toured the USA in 1925–1926 with Olga Baklanova in the title role.
1931	Performed in a translation by Arthur S. Way by the Cambridge Festival Theatre, directed by Terence Gray. Notable for having choreography by Ninette de Valois.
1936	An all-black version in an adaptation by Theodore Brown produced by the Federal Theatre Project at Washington University.
1938	Production of the translation by Benjamin Bickley Rogers which the translator of the Edexcel version cites as the edition he used to base his own translation on. Produced at the Open Air Theatre, Regent's Park with Gladys Cooper as Lysistrata.
1947	Austrian film version entitled *Triumph der Liebe*, directed by Alfred Stöger.
1957	Dudley Fitts' version of the play which brought it to the attention of a wider British audience. First produced at Oxford Playhouse with a one-week tour to Brighton's Theatre Royal, with Constance Cummings in the title role. It also featured Prunella Scales in the role of Myrrhine. The production, directed by Minos Volonakis, was revived by the English Stage Company at the Royal Court Theatre with Joan Greenwood in the title role.

Further reading

You'll find more detailed background information on Ancient Greek Theatre and Aristophanes and his work in the following books:

Bolt, R., *Lysistrata*. Oberon Classics, 2005.

Brown, J. R., ed., *The Oxford Illustrated History of Theatre*. Oxford University Press, 2001.

Einhorn, E., *Lysistrata*. (A version related to the Iraq War). Theater 61 Press, 2007.

Greer, G. and Willmott, P., *Lysistrata: The Sex Strike*. Aurora Metro Press, 2000.

Green, J.R., *Theatre in Ancient Greek Society*. Routledge, 1996.

Harrison, T., *The Common Chorus* (in *Plays 4*). Faber and Faber, 2002. (An adaptation of *Lysistrata* and Euripides' *Women of Troy,* set in Greenham Common at the time of the women's demonstration against nuclear weapons.)

McLeish, K., *Aristophanes: Plays 1 (The Archarnians, The Knights, Peace, Lysistrata)*. Methuen Drama, 1993.

McLeish, K., *Guide to Greek Theatre and Drama*. Methuen, 2003.

Silk, M.S., *Aristophanes and the Definitions of Comedy*. Oxford University Press, 2000.

Sommerstein, A.H., *Greek Drama and Dramatists*. Routledge, 2002.

1961	Broadway musical version entitled *The Happiest Girl in the World* with a script by Fred Saidy and Henry Mayers. The song lyrics were by E.Y. Harburg (famous for *The Wizard of Oz)*. The words were set to the music of Jacques Offenbach. It ran for nearly 100 performances.
1968	Protest version against the Vietnam War written in the style of a Mozart opera by Bob Fink and performed at Wayne State University Opera Workshop. Ironically, the first performance had to be cancelled because one of the lead singers was drafted into the army.
1976	Belgian film version directed by Ludo Mich in which the entire cast is naked to save on the costume budget!
1993	Peter Hall's production using Ranjit Bolt's rhyming couplet translation. Opened at the Playhouse in Liverpool, transferred to London's Old Vic Theatre and then to Wyndham's in the West End. It starred Geraldine James as Lysistrata. It was notable for its contemporary Greek setting by the Greek designer Dionyssis Fotopoulos. The male costumes had baggy trouser fronts which contained an ingenious mechanism allowing the actors to display their erect phalluses.
1999	Germaine Greer's feminist version directed by Phil Willmott at the Battersea Arts Centre. Michael Billington in *The Guardian* described it as 'textual tinkering and a determinedly jokey production that transforms the play from sharp moral satire into a genial Carry On Up The Acropolis.'
2002	*Lisístrata* – a Spanish film version based on the 1987 comic book version of *Lysistrata* by Ralf König in which Lysistrata is portrayed as a lesbian. Hepatitos, leader of Gay Greek United, tries to persuade the men of Athens to have sex with men to counteract the women's sex strike.
2003	On 3 March, over 1,000 readings of *Lysistrata* were held in 59 countries to protest at the threat of war against Iraq organised by Kathryn Blume and Sharron Bower, two actresses from New York City. A documentary film about the project, *Operation Lysistrata,* directed by Michael Patrick Kelly, was released in 2006.
2005	An adaptation written by Jason Tyne set in modern-day New York City was premiered in Central Park. The character of the magistrate was renamed George W. Bush.
2007	Northern Broadsides' new version entitled *Lisa's Sex Strike* written by Blake Morrison and directed by Conrad Nelson. It is set in the North of England amidst racial and ethnic tension. The women hold a sex strike and seize the factory to bring about peace.

DOCTOR FAUSTUS

We don't know exactly when Marlowe's play *Doctor Faustus* was written and first performed, but we do know that it was popular during the Elizabethan period (1558–1603, the reign of Elizabeth I), and that it was first published in 1604.

Doctor Faustus remains a popular play today, at least 400 years after its first appearance. What is its attraction for modern audiences? Why might a 21st-century director find it a stimulating and challenging play to explore?

What do we know about Christopher Marlowe?

As with Shakespeare, we know relatively little about Marlowe, but what we do know tells us that he had a colourful and eventful life, as well as an early and violent death. (His surname appears as Marlin and Morley in some legal and administrative documents – just as with Shakespeare, there were variant spellings of his name in his lifetime.)

Taking it further

You'll find more detailed background information on Marlowe and *Doctor Faustus* in the books listed on page 142.

Timeline

February 1564	Born in Canterbury, the second of nine children, but the oldest to survive infancy. Father is a shoemaker.
1579	Awarded a scholarship at King's School, Canterbury.
December 1580	Awarded a scholarship at Corpus Christi College, Cambridge. Writes *Dido, Queen of Carthage*, poetry and probably *Tamburlaine the Great*.
1585	Awarded BA degree; 1587: Awarded MA degree, but only after the intervention of the Privy Council of Queen Elizabeth on his behalf.
1584–1587	Student at Cambridge, probably working at times as an undercover government agent in Reims, France, gleaning information about possible Catholic plots against the Queen. *Doctor Faustus* possibly written in this period.
September 1589	Living in London, arrested for being involved in a duel in which his friend kills another man.
1590–91	*The Jew of Malta* written and performed.
1592	Arrested for counterfeiting coins in Flushing (Vlissingen, a town in the Netherlands then in the possession of England); possibly imprisoned in London. *Edward II* written and performed, and possibly *The Massacre at Paris*.
Early May 1593	Arrested for fighting with two constables in the street.
18 May 1593	Warrant issued for his arrest on suspicion of atheism.
30 May 1593	Stabbed through the eye socket during a fight in an inn in Deptford, South London. Dies instantly. His killer, Ingram Frizer, is pardoned shortly afterwards. After his death, accusations of atheism, heresy and even homosexuality continue.

The text of the play

You need to be aware of the issues created by the text. There are two different versions, identified now as the 'A' and 'B' Texts. The 'A' Text was published in 1604, 11 years after Marlowe's death. The 'B' Text was published in 1616. It is over 600 lines longer than the 'A' Text, including additional comic scenes, and omits 36 lines which are in the 'A' Text. In addition, there are thousands of minor variations in individual words, phrases and punctuation, some of which make a significant difference to the meaning.

You must use the Edexcel prescribed version of the play in the exam, though you may wish to consult other editions during your research. The prescribed version is taken from the *Norton Critical Edition: Doctor Faustus* by Christopher Marlowe, edited by David Scott Kastan (W.W. Norton & Co., 2005).

A great deal of time has been spent by scholars trying to work out exactly what Marlowe's original text contained. At least one editor, W.W. Greg, produced a '**conjectural**' text of the play, working along these lines. More recent editors have realised that this is a futile exercise – we will never know what Marlowe wrote and it is possible that some of the play was not written by him. (It was common practice in the Elizabethan theatre for plays to be multi-authored.) In 1602, two playwrights, William Bird and Samuel Rowley, were paid by the theatre manager, Philip Henslowe, to make *adicyones* (additions) to the play – but we don't know what these additions were. Note that this was two years before the first publication of the 'A' Text. Recent editions of Marlowe's works have adopted the practice of publishing both versions of the text.

How does this affect you as the student?

If you see a performance of the play at the theatre, you may be surprised to be watching scenes that you have never studied! The version that you are studying is the 'A' Text. If you use another edition of the play while preparing for the exam (for example, to refer to notes), you should ensure that it is an 'A' Text edition.

Synopsis of the 'A' Text

Doctor Faustus, a distinguished teacher at the University of Wittenberg in Germany, declares his dissatisfaction with academic learning and decides to devote himself to the study of magic. He summons up the evil spirit Mephistopheles, and proposes a contract (later signed in his blood) in which he trades his soul for 24 years during which Mephistopheles will be his servant, answer all his questions and give him whatever he wants. Mephistopheles gives him a book containing the secrets of the universe.

Later, Faustus has doubts, but despite being urged by the Good Angel, is unable to repent. Lucifer appears and distracts him with a parade of the Seven Deadly Sins. Faustus (invisibly) visits the Pope's court where he mocks and plays practical jokes on him. He visits the Emperor of Constantinople and 'resurrects' Alexander the Great for him. Later, after playing a practical joke on a horse-dealer, he 'resurrects' Helen of Troy for three fellow scholars.

In the final scene, which takes place during the last hour of the 24 years, Faustus is struck with terror at the thought of his eternal damnation, but cannot bring about his own repentance. After the clock strikes midnight, devils appear to drag him off to hell.

Key term

conjectural

Edexcel Examiner's tip

You must ensure that you have the prescribed text from Edexcel. This version has space for you to write notes and the examiner will be referring to the same version – if you use page numbers from a different version in the exam, the examiner will not know which lines you are referring to. Only the prescribed version will be permitted in the exam room.

Social, cultural and historical context

For both Section A and Section B of the exam, you will answer questions on the play from the point of view of a director. Any director of the play today needs to understand the context of the original play – not to try to recreate it in a modern production, but to see how it has relevance to society now. Specific decisions about rehearsals and the production will be affected by this knowledge.

We do not know exactly when the first performance of *Doctor Faustus* was, but it was almost certainly at the Rose Theatre on the South Bank of the Thames in London, and may well have been in 1589. What do we know about the audience who would have seen it there? How different were they from us in their ways of life and their beliefs?

The Elizabethan audience

The audience was very mixed socially. Plays of the kind written by Shakespeare and Marlowe were a relatively new form of entertainment (the first purpose-built theatre arrived in 1576 – called, unsurprisingly, 'The Theatre'), and theatre-going became a popular activity amongst all social classes. It cost one old penny (1d – the cost of a loaf of bread or a pint of beer) to stand as a 'groundling' and watch the play. If you were wealthier, you could pay more for well-placed seats with cushions. The poorest inhabitants of London could not afford to go. Both men and women watched plays, but only males were allowed to act in them. The Queen did not go to public theatres, however; the plays came to her.

What were their lives like?

The conditions of life were a good deal harsher than our own. Life expectancy was between 32 and 40. Many children did not survive childbirth or infancy (three of Marlowe's siblings did not). Outbreaks of the bubonic plague (the 'Black Death') were fairly common and these caused large numbers of deaths. Other diseases (typhus, malaria, tuberculosis) were also killers. Reminders of death were everywhere, and the Elizabethans accepted death as a stage on the way to the after-life; how you spent your life determined your fate after the body's death.

Life could be uncomfortable: there was no sewage system, so streets were messy and smelly places. The provisions for personal hygiene were negligible by our standards. (The 'groundlings' were also known as the 'stinkards', especially during the summer, for obvious reasons.)

Punishments for crimes were harsh. These included public executions, with the bodies of those hanged often left to rot on gibbets, or their severed heads placed in public places such as bridges or on the spikes on the tops of gates. These were the normal conditions of life and people did not protest against them. They did not go to the theatre to see their own lives reflected on stage; they went to see representations of very different lives.

The importance of religion

Religion played an important part in people's lives and Marlowe's play should be seen in this context. The average Elizabethan would have had no doubt at all about the existence of the soul, heaven and hell, salvation and damnation.

Atheists (or 'freethinkers') were in a tiny minority, and the majority of Elizabethans believed in orthodox religion.

The 16th century had seen huge changes in what religion meant. Henry VIII had broken from the Roman Catholic Church in 1534, and established the Protestant Church of England. After his death in 1547, the state religion changed to extreme Protestantism under his son, Edward VI, then reverted to Roman Catholicism under his daughter, Mary, then changed to moderate Protestantism under his younger daughter, Elizabeth I. By the time Marlowe was writing plays, there were strong anti-Catholic laws in place, but many Elizabethans still secretly believed that Roman Catholicism was the true Christian religion. Religion was a live issue.

Marlowe himself was probably spying for the Government, looking for Roman Catholic 'terrorists' during the periods when he went missing from his studies at Cambridge (see page 87). (Remember that the Gunpowder Plot of 1605 was a Catholic plot to blow up the Houses of Parliament.) The scene in *Doctor Faustus* when Faustus and Mephistopheles make themselves invisible and play practical jokes on the Pope in Rome no doubt went down well with an audience who had been encouraged to see the Pope as a money-grabbing, self-indulgent tyrant.

The rise of self-improvement

People were becoming more educated. Henry VIII had made laws encouraging people to become more literate, although the ability to read and write was still largely confined to the higher social classes. The ability to read and interpret the Bible for themselves meant that people would become less dependent on the Catholic tradition of priests interpreting the word of God for them. Printed books were becoming more widespread and cheaper. People were encouraged to better themselves economically. Marlowe's father, a shoemaker, learnt to read and write as an adult and developed his income by undertaking some legal work and work as a clerk.

The spirit of enquiry

During the Renaissance there was a growing sense of human beings expanding their knowledge and asking questions about the world and the universe. There was still a strong sense, however, that people should 'know their place' and not go beyond the boundaries set for them by God. There was a strong belief that God would intervene to punish sinners in this world as well as the next; a number of Marlowe's enemies regarded his death as a punishment from God for expressing unorthodox views about religion.

> The Renaissance (literally 'rebirth') is the period from roughly the 14th to 17th centuries, in which classical Greek and Roman learning was rediscovered in Western Europe and there was a growing interest in science, art, literature, philosophy and other branches of learning. The phrase 'Renaissance man', although not used until the 20th century, refers to a person who has developed a wide range of learning, but continually strives for more. In this sense, Faustus is a true 'Renaissance man'; he has mastered a number of important branches of learning such as law, medicine, philosophy and religion, but is still hungry for more knowledge.

Taking it further

Read the longer version of the scene with the Pope in the 'B' Text of the play, in which the rival Pope, Bruno, is introduced, and the anti-Catholic feeling is made even clearer.

Note that Faustus comes from humble origins ('his parents base of stock', Prologue, line 11) and rises to great heights.

Taking it further

For more information about politics, religion, literature and the theatre, look at Stevie Simkin's book *Marlowe* (Chapter 2, 'The Time of Marlowe').

Performance history

The earliest performances

There are no records of the early performances of *Doctor Faustus*, but we know that it was a popular play in the period immediately after Marlowe's death. We know also that the part of Faustus was played by Edward Alleyn, one of the greatest actors of the time.

We have little real evidence about the style of acting during Marlowe's lifetime, although we can make some guesses. Then, as now, there may have been different styles of acting associated with different companies and playhouses. One important feature was the fact that the audience was completely visible to the actors. Performances in public playhouses (such as the Rose, Globe and Swan) started at 2 p.m. in broad daylight.

The thrust stage common to most of these playhouses pushed the actors out towards the audience. The closest members of the audience to the actors were the 'groundlings', who were sometimes rowdy and disruptive. It was in the actors' interests to ensure that their presence was acknowledged. In comedies, this would mean that jokes were shared with the audience (some comic players were skilled improvisers); in tragedies, the **soliloquies** were probably 'shared' with the audience. Audiences were quite large – most public theatres of this period could accommodate at least 2,000 in the audience, and some up to 3,500 – far bigger than any current West End theatre!

> **Key term**
>
> soliloquy

Less time was spent in rehearsal than in our day, and actors were only given copies of their own parts (and cues), not the whole play. The idea of interpreting a whole play is likely to have been very different, especially as there was no 'director' in the sense that we understand it. The notion that a director could have a 'concept' or 'interpretation' of the text (an idea which is extremely relevant to you on this course) would be unknown to them. Although performers would have been skilled, they would not have shared our concept of 'psychological **naturalism**' (which we associate with Stanislavski), and performances would probably have been bigger and broader than in the modern theatre.

Although the decoration of theatres would have been quite ornate, the stage itself was quite bare with minimal use of settings and furniture, so that the actors (using their skill and the text of the play) had to encourage the audience members to use their imaginations.

Despite this, productions of *Doctor Faustus* were accompanied by some spectacular effects. We know that a 'dragon' appeared on stage in the play (it is found in a list of theatre props in 1598, as well as on the title page of an edition printed in 1624), and John Melton, a theatre-goer in 1620 wrote in his book *The Astrologaster* that he saw 'shaggy-haired devils run roaring over the stage with squibs [fire-crackers] in their mouths, while drummers make thunder in the tiring-house [the dressing-room] and the twelve-penny hirelings make lightning in their heavens' (quoted in David Riggs's *The World of Christopher Marlowe*, page 237). The play was popular because it gave opportunities for spectacles like these.

Structure, style and genre

Structure

The structure of *Doctor Faustus* involves a very distinct beginning, middle and end, and is related to time.

Section 1:	
Beginning	We see Faustus making his pact with the Devil, agreeing that he will have access to whatever he desires for a period of 24 years and then will yield up his soul to the Devil.
Section 2:	
Middle	We see how he spends that period of 24 years, partly in gaining knowledge and partly in living for pleasure.
Section 3:	
End	We see the last hours of his life, when the clock strikes midnight at the end of the 24 years and he is dragged down to hell by devils.

There is a Chorus, which 'frames' the action of the play by appearing before and after the main body of the play.

Prologue	This explains:
	• that the audience is about to see a different kind of play from some others recently performed
	• how Faustus was brought up and educated
	• how he turns from his studies to necromancy, which resulted in his 'overthrow'
	• that the character now on stage is, in fact, Faustus.
Epilogue	This explains:
	• that Faustus is 'gone' (i.e. to hell) and that his potentially good life has been brought to an early end
	• that wise members of the audience will see his story as a warning not to follow his example in exceeding the limits laid down for them by heaven.

There are two further appearances by the Chorus (which was probably played by the actor playing Wagner). These (identified as 'Chorus 2' and 'Chorus 3') occur after Act 2 Scene 3 and Act 3 Scene 3, and simply provide narrative links.

The narrative is punctuated by four appearances of the Good and Bad Angels. These can be seen as external representations of the internal forces at work in Faustus' mind; they are also a feature of the medieval **morality plays**. They occur in Act 1 Scene 1, Act 2 Scene 1 and twice in Act 2 Scene 3.

The play has a single narrative line – it follows the story of one man – but there are also scenes which provide a comic parallel to the main story line (Act 1 Scene 4; Act 2 Scene 2; Act 3 Scene 2). They do not add up to a sub-plot, but they provide a comic contrast to the more serious scenes, and a parallel to the scenes in which Faustus and Mephistopheles play practical jokes on the Pope and the Horse-courser. The obviously comic scenes feature Robin and Rafe, parts clearly intended for knockabout comedians. Their desire to use magical powers to enrich themselves and to gain sexual favours from local women represents a debased version of Faustus's intentions.

Style

The play is a mixture of **blank verse** and prose. In plays of this period, comic scenes are often in prose and more serious scenes in blank verse; this is the general pattern in *Doctor Faustus*. Marlowe considerably developed the use and flexibility of blank verse. It was a relatively new form in Marlowe's time, having been first used in poetry in English in 1554 (and not until 1561 in a play). Shakespeare continued the development, and became the finest exponent of it as a medium for drama.

In *Doctor Faustus*, Marlowe uses blank verse for both rhetorical and lyrical effects. 'Rhetorical' means the kind of effects which we associate with the making of formal speeches; Faustus' final speech in the play's last scene is a good example. 'Lyrical' is to do with poetry in which feelings are expressed and the words often possess a musical quality. Faustus' speech to the vision of Helen ('Was this the face that launched a thousand ships...?') demonstrates this quality.

The mixture of the 'high seriousness' for which blank verse could be used, and the more down-to-earth qualities of everyday language in prose became a feature of plays of this period.

Genre

There are two distinct **genres** in *Doctor Faustus*, and one of the key issues for a modern director is what weight to give to each of them. Marlowe combines features from the old morality play tradition with those from the more recent fashion of tragedy. The list of productions on page 100 shows how very different approaches have been taken by later directors.

Many people in Marlowe's day watched morality plays for entertainment. These plays were popular in the 14th to 16th centuries, and aimed to teach a moral lesson. The characters are usually representative, either of humanity (e.g. Everyman) or of various vices and virtues (Mercy, Mischief, Good Deeds). They show a spiritual journey often in the form of an actual journey in which the central figure is presented with choices and temptations but eventually, by the grace of God, wins through to heaven.

The developing form of tragedy involved the story of a great or potentially great man whose downfall and death are brought about by his own actions (which are overambitious, ill-judged or extreme). It did not draw any obvious or simple moral from this story, but often attracted sympathy for the central character.

Marlowe uses elements from the old morality plays in *Doctor Faustus*. The Seven Deadly Sins are clearly drawn from this tradition as representative figures. The Good and Bad Angels are also representative figures, presenting Faustus with a choice by externalising his inner conflict. The virtuous Old Man who appears towards the end of the play is a similar figure from the morality play tradition.

There are also elements of the more modern tragedy in *Doctor Faustus*. Faustus clearly feels frustrated by the limitations imposed on him as a man; he aspires to knowledge and power and boldly decides to gain them, whatever the cost may be to himself. Do we see Faustus as a man who gets what he deserves for sinning against the will of God – or do we see him as a noble and tragic figure, destroyed by his excessive (but understandable) thirst for knowledge?

Key terms

blank verse
genre

Blank verse

In rehearsal, a director should ensure that the actors understand that the way the verse is written is part of the meaning; the rhythms, the pauses, the punctuation and the split lines are all aids to the actor. It is important to recognise that it is not a naturalistic way of speaking, even though it has a strong link with the natural rhythms of spoken English. It does demand a 'heightened' style of speech, which prose does not always require.

Taking it further

The following books contain information on the speaking of blank verse:
Berry, C., *The Actor and the Text*. Harrap, 2000.
Rodenburg, P., *Speaking Shakespeare*. Palgrave Macmillan, 2002.
Barton, J., *Playing Shakespeare*. A & C Black, 1984.

Research

Rehearsal techniques

In Section A of the exam, you will be asked to write about your ideas for rehearsals (with reference to a given extract from the play). Your techniques as a director will depend on the approach you are taking and your production concept. You may also have the approach of a particular practitioner in mind; references to appropriate practitioners should enrich your answers.

Characters and relationships

If you are taking a naturalistic approach to the play, you may want to employ techniques which are designed to explore character and relationships in some depth. Techniques such as hot-seating, thought-tracking, given circumstances, imagination and emotion memory will be of interest to you and your team (see the 'Characterisation' section on pages 49–52 of the AS Student Book).

You will need to decide whether it is sensible to apply some of these 'psychological' techniques (such as those of Stanislavski) to representative characters: does it make any sense to think of the Good and Bad Angels, The Seven Deadly Sins or the Old Man as 'characters'? These are not naturalistic characters, but representative or symbolic characters from the morality play tradition. You may wish to focus your attention on physical and vocal exaggeration, or on the creation of a modern stereotype, rather than aim for a fully rounded, psychologically complex character.

Objectives

You will probably want your actors to clarify what their characters' intentions are, and to understand clearly why they do what they do. You may wish to help them define 'units' (or the sections to which a particular objective applies), or break this down further, using the technique of **actioning** (see page 47 of the AS Student Book).

> **Key term**
>
> actioning

Voice, movement, physical theatre

You will want your cast to use a wide range of their voice and movement abilities, so (as well as using appropriate warm-ups) you may wish to devise games and physical and vocal improvisations to help them explore the limits of their role. You can invent your own activities exploring the potential of the text in physical and vocal terms. Isolating physical or vocal qualities and exaggerating these can help actors to discover things about their roles and relationships.

Text and sub-text

Understanding both of these is important, although sub-text is a less obvious feature of texts of this period. Slow reading can be helpful: ask your cast to read through the text very slowly (with no attempt to perform or interpret) so that every word is considered and, if necessary, discussed.

Acting style and practitioners

Style is a difficult concept to discuss and is often easier to deal with in practice in the rehearsal room. From what we know about the general approach to acting in Marlowe's time, we may assume that characterisation was broader and larger, and that gestures and movements were more standardised as 'signals' to the audience. All acting styles will find a place somewhere on the line between 'extreme naturalism' and 'extreme non-naturalism'.

Your decisions about style will be affected if you are influenced by a particular practitioner: for example, followers of Stanislavski may focus on the personal tragedy of Faustus and his relationship with Mephistopheles; a Brechtian interpretation may see a political element in the play and wish to confront the audience with this; the play may lend itself to some of Artaud's ideas, leaving the audience powerfully affected by theatrical shocks; Grotowski's version of the play saw Faustus as the doomed hero, struggling against an unjust God.

Activity 1

Take a scene from the play and act it out in an unexpected style.

It's interesting (and positive, energising fun) to rehearse scenes in the style of *EastEnders* melodrama, for example, or a Quentin Tarantino film. You can try rewriting the text in modern English so it's appropriate to the style. This activity can often bring out particular character qualities or 'unlock' something in an actor.

Directing *Doctor Faustus*

Firstly, you will need to make some major decisions in order to have a clear view of your own production. Your detailed decisions in rehearsal will follow on logically from these decisions. In your practical work on the text, you will be able to explore how your decisions will affect specific scenes and moments in the play, and determine what kind of interpretation yours could be.

Morality play or tragedy?

Marlowe's play has elements of both genres. As a director, which do you wish to emphasise in your production? Do you see the play as the story of a man who sins against the will of God and is punished accordingly, or do you see Faustus as a man of intellectual and moral stature who defies the restricting rules of his time and heroically stands out against them? Or will your production be somewhere in between these two extremes?

Activity 2

Read the section 'Faustus' last moments' on page 99. Experiment with different ways of presenting the last few moments of the play, trying first to stress the 'morality play' aspects of the play, and then to stress the 'heroic' aspects of Faustus.

How will you deal with the comedy?

It has been suggested that the comedy elements could not have been written by Marlowe as they were not 'worthy' of such a great play. Some directors have omitted the broader comic scenes, saying that they 'trivialise' the play. You need to decide how the comic and the more serious elements work together in the play. Some comic scenes don't involve Faustus (the Robin and Rafe scenes), but some do (the scenes set at the Pope's Court in Rome, the Emperor's Court and with the Horse-courser). Are the Robin and Rafe scenes meant to reflect elements of the main story line? If so, how? Do you see them as a contrast to Faustus' story or as an ironic comment on it?

In your practical work, you can experiment with creating visual and verbal 'echoes' between these scenes, creating links in the audience's minds (for example, by placing characters in similar positions on stage, or adopting similar body shapes or vocal characteristics).

How spectacular will your production be?

The play was popular in the 17th century because it provided opportunities for spectacular effects. How do these effects relate to your ideas about the play as a whole? If Faustus has the power to create astonishing effects, do you think he has gained powers worth having? Do the effects of Mephistopheles' creating (and the opening of hell's mouth at the end) demonstrate the frightening power of the darker forces? You may be able to create simple but striking effects using sound and lighting – or possibly fireworks, as long as you're aware of health and safety issues. You can certainly develop more ambitious plans without actually putting them into practice.

How will you view Faustus and Mephistopheles' relationship?

How genuinely close and 'equal' is their relationship? Barry Kyle's 1989 production suggested a homoerotic relationship between Faustus and Mephistopheles, and other productions have used the suggestions in the text of an affinity and sympathy between the two characters. Both, however, have different goals; Mephistopheles aims to win Faustus' soul by condemning him to eternal damnation. Will you present him as cynically exploiting a naive Faustus, or as having genuine sympathy for him, while having to do a job for which he has little enthusiasm? All their scenes together can be explored by giving the actor playing Mephistopheles different objectives to pursue.

Mephistopheles and Faustus in simple, modern style – 2004 Chichester Festival

Will you adapt the text?

As mentioned on page 88, it is impossible to establish what Marlowe actually wrote; as a result, directors have felt more free than usual to cut, change and adapt the text. Your job is to imagine yourself as director of the Edexcel version of the 'A' Text. Remember that you have the freedom that any director has to edit this text, or to add to the stage directions.

Which stage form will you choose?

This is a vital decision, as much of the potential of your production will be governed by it. The most common forms are end-on (often proscenium arch), in-the-round, thrust or traverse. Refer back to pages 147–152 of the AS Student Book where the advantages and potential problems of these are discussed. The actor–audience relationship will be a factor in your choice.

More inventive staging solutions are also possible: Grotowski's 1963 production had the audience seated at two long, plain tables, like monks in the refectory of a monastery, with Faustus sitting at a smaller table set at the head of the longer ones. The stage form has to provide the right vehicle for your ideas about the play; you need to be able to justify and explain your choice.

What will the stage area be like?

This links closely with your decision about stage form. Does your production need a lot of space? Or do you want the playing space to be as small as possible so that the cast are interacting with very little space between them? The question of actor–audience relationship is important here.

When making decisions about stage form and playing space, you must be aware of two important factors:

- Technical and set requirements: if you want Faustus's study to have walls covered with loaded bookshelves, then in-the-round will be the wrong choice. If you want to project a vision of hell opening to receive Faustus, then you'll need a screen or wall to project it onto.

- Scene changes: plays from this period were written to flow continuously, without gaps between the scenes. If you want to maintain this flow of action, you need to ensure that any necessary scene changes (such as removing or setting tables, desks, thrones) don't hold up the pace.

Period or contemporary?

Plays have to be set in time and space. You must decide whether you wish to treat the play as belonging to the period in which it was set (about 1590 originally), or whether you want to transfer it to another period (which could include today).

One extreme is 'museum theatre' (an obsession with replicating the conditions of the original period), and the other extreme is an insistence on ensuring that the maximum degree of contemporary relevance is wrung out of the play. Both approaches have their potential strengths and weaknesses.

It is clear, though, that a production taking place today needs to engage an audience of today. Two productions have tried to link J. Robert Oppenheimer (the inventor of the nuclear bomb) with Faustus: Marowitz's 1969 production and John Adams's 2005 opera version, *Doctor Atomic*. These productions drew specific parallels, but more general parallels can be made by setting the play in a particular period or society. Grotowski's setting in a monastery (1963) related to his concept of Faustus as a kind of modern saint, challenging the power of an immoral god.

You may find good reasons for setting *Doctor Faustus* in the Victorian period, the First World War, the 1960s, or the 21st century. You may have reasons for setting it in the United States, China, India, or any other country. The important thing is that those reasons justify your choice.

Think it through

Once you've made these bigger decisions, you must think through the impact of each of them on all of the other details of the production. Productions of plays always pose practical problems which directors and creative teams have to solve. In your work on the play for this exam, you will not be limited by practical and financial constraints as you might in a real production situation.

If you opt for today as your setting, you may find difficulty in deciding on appropriate props. What do you do when Mephistopheles has to bring in 'a chafer of coals' (Act 2 Scene 1)? Do you use a cigarette lighter as a reasonable modern substitute? If you opt for a modern version of Faustus's study, will he need to be hooked up to the internet?

You will have to make decisions about the appearance of Mephistopheles, Beelzebub and the other devils. Faustus is quite specific in instructing Mephistopheles to appear as 'an old Franciscan friar', and the stage direction indicates that he does so. You will have to find a suitable appearance for Mephistopheles, which will be acceptable to an audience.

As well as carrying your concept through to costume, set and props, you will have to consider the behaviour of the actors. Certain types of movement and speech are associated with particular periods of time and with particular social settings. Your actors may have to learn the manners, physical bearing and speech habits which go with that society and period. For example, greetings are important – bows, hand-shakes, kissing of hands – and these vary between the genders from period to period. Also, until the 20th century women, when seated would never cross their legs. The costume of any period is important as it could restrict movement in certain ways. Very precise, clipped diction was a feature of the upper and upper-middle classes of the first half of the 20th century.

Key moments

These are likely to be the moments of most intense drama where decisions are made or climaxes are reached. How you handle these will be a vital part of how you see the play and how you want your audience to respond to it. Here are some examples of how directors have handled some key moments in the past.

Faustus' last moments

"Faustus finished his final speech grovelling in abject terror on the ground. The clock finished striking. Nothing happened. After a long moment Faustus raised his head and looked around the totally empty stage. He started to laugh. As he reached the hysteria of relief, the back wall of the stage gave way and fell forward in sections revealing an ominous red glow and a set of spikes like the dragon's teeth of the Siegfried Line. The denizens of hell emerged with a kind of slow continuous shuffle until Faustus was surrounded by a circle of those skeletal figures – including the Seven Deadly Sins. He was then seized and carried shrieking through the teeth of hell mouth which closed leaving the wall of Faustus' study again intact."

Nigel Alexander describing Clifford Williams' production for the Royal Shakespeare Company in 1968 (in Stevie Simkin's Marlowe, *page 123)*

The director's organisation of the pause in which Faustus believes for a moment that nothing will happen to him, followed by the frightening vision of hell and his damnation, adds a powerful twist to the final moments. Contrast this with Grotowski's 1963 production in which the final speech was played as 'his last and most outrageous provocation of God'. Faustus was played as a 'saint' going towards his 'martyrdom'.

Taking it further

Read more about Grotowski's interpretation of the play in *The Grotowski Sourcebook*, edited by Richard Schechner and Lisa Wolford (Routledge, 1997).

"Mephistopheles lugs Faustus away on his back, holding him by the feet, the saint's head down near the ground, his hands trailing on the floor. He goes to his eternal damnation as a sacrificial animal is carried, as one is dragged to the Cross ... He is the victor, morally. But he has played the full price of that victory: eternal martyrdom in hell, where all is taken from him, even his dignity."

Eugenio Barba in The Grotowski Sourcebook *(pages 62– 63)*

Activity 3

Consider the following key moments in the play and think about what different approaches might be taken to each of them in order to emphasise different elements of the scene:

a) The first appearance of Mephistopheles

b) The second appearance of Mephistopheles (as 'an old Franciscan friar')

c) The making of the pact/cutting Faustus's arm

d) The appearance of Beelzebub and Lucifer.

Interpretation

Although many people no longer believe in a literal devil and hell in the way that Marlowe's contemporaries would have done, this doesn't mean that the play won't work today. Many recent productions have shown how well the play still works and how fascinating its central idea remains. Every period of time has reinvented Faustus in various ways. The intriguing challenge for you as a director is to find a way of making the play powerful, dramatic and relevant to an audience today.

Doctor Faustus has been performed in many different versions. It is interesting for potential directors to see how different productions (or versions) have emphasised different elements in the original story. These highlight the areas for directorial choice – an issue which is relevant to you as you decide on your own interpretation.

1662	New version of Marlowe's play performed with additional/changed scenes. The scene at the Pope's court is changed and relocated to Babylon to avoid offending Roman Catholic sympathisers in Charles II's court. The spectacular elements were also emphasised, with Faustus moving trees and raising armies of devils.
1675–1896	No performances of Marlowe's *Doctor Faustus* during this period of more than two centuries (but see below).
1697	A 'pantomime' version, *The Life and Death of Doctor Faustus, Made into a Farce, with the Humours of Harlequin and Scaramouche*, published. This strongly emphasised the comedy.
1724	*The Harlequin Doctor Faustus* by John Thurmond continues this tradition with comic set pieces and expensive spectacular effects. Faustus becomes a character often seen in pantomimes at this time.
1896	Marlowe's original text is revived by William Poel for the Elizabethan Stage Society on a replica of the Elizabethan Fortune Theatre's stage.
1929	*Doctor Faustus* appears on a double bill with *Everyman* (one of the best-known medieval morality plays) at the first ever Canterbury Festival. It was interpreted as a morality play, portraying Faustus as a sinner who came to a deserved end.
1937	Orson Welles directs a heavily cut version of the play and plays Faustus himself, casting a black actor (Jack Carter) as Mephistopheles. This production emphasises the idea that Faustus was a doomed genius, and Welles (a keen amateur magician) ensures that there are strikingly spectacular effects, as well as some slapstick comedy.
1963	Jerzy Grotowski, the influential Polish director, in a 'montage' version of the play (i.e. selected parts, not necessarily played in order), portrays Faustus as a tragic hero: 'the martyr of a spiteful deity'.
1965	Richard Burton plays Faustus and Elizabeth Taylor plays Helen (and other female roles) in a stage version at the Oxford Playhouse and later in a film version. Faustus is seen as torn between his desires and his sense of guilt; the film also has what were at the time spectacular special effects.

1968	Clifford Williams's production of the play at the Royal Shakespeare Company is notable for showing the various apparitions (such as Helen of Troy and the Seven Deadly Sins) as they really are (grotesque and ugly), not as they are seen by Faustus. The effect is to make the audience aware of the way in which Faustus is being deceived.
1969	Charles Marowitz directs a 'collage' version with a specially written prologue making parallels between Faustus and J. Robert Oppenheimer, the inventor of the nuclear bomb, who later denounced the use his invention was being put to.
1974	Ian McKellen plays Faustus in a version which takes place entirely in Faustus' study, with the Good and Bad Angels and the Seven Deadly Sins being played by hand puppets. The effect is to suggest that the entire play is taking place in Faustus' mind.
1989	Barry Kyle's production suggests a homoerotic relationship between Faustus and Mephistopheles.
2002	Jude Law plays Faustus at The Young Vic (London) as one of a cast of seven (all males) on a traverse stage. This involves some doubling, with Faustus himself taking the part of Pride in the appearance of the Seven Deadly Sins.
2006	Punchdrunk's site-specific promenade production, played on five floors of a disused warehouse in Wapping, is strong on seedy atmosphere; 1950s America inspires the design for this very physical production.
2006	Headlong Theatre's version (with added modern scenes) parallels Faustus' story with that of the Chapman Brothers, cutting-edge modern artists who intentionally defaced priceless prints made by the artist Goya with faces of smiling teddy bears, etc.
2008	Third Party Productions uses a cast of three, varying the order of the text (and adding some lines) to produce a version which emphasises Faustus' stupidity and gullibility, balancing comedy against the tragic elements.
2009	At the ICA in London, Akhe Engineering Theatre (from Russia) perform a version entitled *Faust. 2360 Words*, a highly visual and inventive version (using exactly 2360 words), again featuring only three actors – and live chemistry experiments on stage.

Further reading

You'll find more detailed background information on Marlowe and *Doctor Faustus* in the following books:

Bevington, D., and Rasmussen, E., eds., *The Revels Plays: Doctor Faustus*, A- and B-Texts (1604, 1616). Manchester University Press, 1993.

Cheney, P., ed., *The Cambridge Companion to Christopher Marlowe*. Cambridge University Press, 2004.

Gill, R., ed., *Doctor Faustus*. A & C Black, 2003.

Hopkins, L., *Christopher Marlowe: Renaissance Dramatist*. Edinburgh University Press, 2008.

Jump, J., ed., *Marlowe: Doctor Faustus*. Palgrave Macmillan Casebook, 1969.

Mangan, M., *Doctor Faustus*. Penguin Critical Studies, 1989.

Oz, A., ed., *New Casebooks: Marlowe*. Palgrave Macmillan, 2004.

Riggs, D., *The World of Christopher Marlowe*. Faber and Faber, 2004.

Simkin, S., *Marlowe*. Longman Preface Books, 2000.

Useful website:
http://www.theatron.org

WOYZECK

Taking it further

You'll find more detailed background information on Büchner and *Woyzeck* in the books listed on page 152.

Woyzeck was probably written in 1836 by Georg Büchner; he died a year later, aged 23, apparently leaving the play unfinished. We do not know exactly when Büchner wrote the play, nor do we know if the versions we have today are what Büchner intended for the full play; scholars have never agreed on even the order of the scenes within the play. Nobody knows how the writer wanted his play to be read or performed, so it's up to you how you are going to interpret it. As a result, *Woyzeck* remains a challenge to contemporary directors and has formed the basis for some exciting interpretations on stage and in film.

What do we know about Georg Büchner?

Timeline

17 October 1813	Born in Goddelau in the grand Duchy of Hesse-Darmstadt, an independent state in what is now Germany. He is the son of a doctor and the first of six children.
1822–1831	Educated privately and then at the Gymnasium in Darmstadt.
1831–1833	Studies zoology and comparative anatomy in Strassburg, another independent German state. He becomes politically aware through contact with a radical student group. During this time he becomes engaged to Wilhelmine (Minna) Jaeglé, the daughter of his landlord.
1833	Returns to Hesse to study at the University of Giessen, where he suffers an attack of meningitis.
1834	Helps establish the Society of Human Rights and co-writes an illegal pamphlet called 'The Hessian Courier', with Pastor Weidig. The pamphlet is critical of social conditions in Hesse. He is denounced by the authorities, but denies authorship and escapes arrest. He returns home to Darmstadt. Pastor Weidig is arrested, tortured and dies in prison.
January to February 1835	Secretly writes Danton's Death in just five weeks, dramatising the thoughts and actions of the political activist Danton, around the time of the French Revolution.
March 1835	Flees to Strassburg, closely avoiding arrest for political activism. Writes and publishes Lenz, a novel based on the life of the poet of the same name. It is quickly banned.
1836	Publishes a dissertation, Mémoire sur le Système Nerveux du Barbeaux, a paper about the nervous system of the barb fish, and he receives his doctorate. Later he gives a successful trial lecture about the cranial nerves of these fish, and is appointed Lecturer in Anatomy at the University of Zurich.
	The same year he writes Leonce and Lena, a comedy about royalty and how freedom is limited by society's moral and social conventions. He enters the play too late for a competition and it is returned to him.
	Probably in the summer, he begins writing his best known play, posthumously given the title Woyzeck. He creates four drafts of the play.
19 February 1837	Contracts typhus and after battling the illness for 17 days, dies from it. He is 23 years old.
1878–1879	The four drafts of the play we now know as Woyzeck are published as Wozzeck. This is a reworked version by Karl Emil Franzos. Intellectuals hotly debate the order of the scenes and which version is the 'final' one.
1896	Leonce and Lena first performed to a German audience.
8 November 1913	First performance of Woyzeck at the Residenztheater, Munich

The text of the play

The text you are studying is a translation of Büchner's original German and other translations may differ considerably. While it's crucial that you use the Edexcel text in the exam, this does not mean that you have to leave the scenes exactly as they are in that edition. If you play the scenes in a different order, what would that do to the meaning you create for your audience?

If you see a production of *Woyzeck*, you may find that the version staged is not exactly the same as the Edexcel edition. The opportunity to experience a director's ideas for an interpretation will still be useful.

Synopsis

Franz Woyzeck is a soldier who has fathered an illegitimate son with his girlfriend, Marie. He is a poor man and has a soldier friend called Andres. There is a fairground scene involving animals and a Showman, and Woyzeck's girlfriend, Marie, becomes very taken with a Drum-Major.

Woyzeck earns extra pay by working for a Captain who finds him stupid and amoral because he is poor. He thinks a poor man could never be virtuous. He also agrees to take part in paid medical experiments that are carried out on him by the Doctor. For one of these, the Doctor tells Woyzeck he must eat nothing except peas in order to prove some unspecified scientific theory. Woyzeck begins to lose his sanity, has a series of visions and suffers from paranoia. The Doctor parades him in front of his students, convincing everyone that Woyzeck is going insane as a result of female upbringing, using the German language and the diet of peas.

Meanwhile Woyzeck's girlfriend, Marie, begins an affair with the Drum-Major. She eventually gives in to him in an ambiguous scene that could disguise her actual rape. The Captain informs Woyzeck of Marie's indiscretions. Woyzeck confronts Marie in a rage. He is driven even more angry when he sees Marie and her lover dancing together, and eventually starts to hear voices telling him to stab her. The Drum-Major beats up Woyzeck in a fight.

Woyzeck buys a knife from a Jewish merchant. He lures Marie to the woods and stabs her, but is quickly found out because he is covered in blood. He runs back to her body and takes it to a nearby pool, then presumably drowns.

The Doctor carries out postmortem examinations on both the bodies, and finds that Woyzeck's corpse has no blood left in it. When Andres returns to the woods where Woyzeck dies, he finds the ground running with blood.

In some translations there is said to have been a final trial scene. Büchner's own notes show Woyzeck getting rid of the knife in the pool, then, as in one of the film versions and most staged ones, he dumps the knife in the water and drowns himself while cleaning off the blood. In the Edexcel version of the text we are not told what he does with the knife; we only see him dragging the body down to the pool's side.

The real Woyzeck

We know that Woyzeck was a real person, a German wig maker and barber, who was executed after stabbing his wife. Büchner became fascinated with this case, which was discussed in medical journals at the time, and used it as inspiration for his own play. Büchner has added characters in the play who are not in the original story, but many of those involved retain their real names.

Social, cultural and historical context

For both Section A and Section B of the exam, you will answer questions on the play from the point of view of a director. Any director of the play today needs to understand the context of the original play – not to try to recreate it in a modern production, but to see how it has relevance to society now. Specific decisions about rehearsals and the production will be affected by this knowledge.

When *Woyzeck* was written

Büchner was born during a time of much political and social unrest in Europe, following the French Revolution at the end of the 18th century and the subsequent Napoleonic Wars which resulted in a loss of two million lives by the time they ended in 1815. Büchner's interest in these events is clear not only from his own revolutionary activities, but also from the content of his writings; his first play *Danton's Death* is about Georges Danton, a leader in the French Revolution.

Key terms

Stürm und Drang
modernism
absurdist
everyman

Büchner was influenced by the **Stürm und Drang** ('Storm and Stress') movement that had been prevalent in Germany in the late 18th century. This was a movement of young male writers who were concerned with the trials and tribulations of the ordinary, common man. Woyzeck is just such a character. Their work was political and quite revolutionary in its content, but unlike writers in France at the time, they did not call for revolution; instead they used their writing to expose hypocrisy and social injustice, often harking back to some mythical time when the world was a better, more natural place.

This play has been called the first truly modern drama; its politics can be seen in the works of Bertolt Brecht, and the style of the play is reflected in many works that were to follow in the **modernist**, **expressionist**, **absurdist** and **naturalistic** theatre forms. This gives the play an importance in theatre history. The idea of the **'everyman'** character can be seen in Dostoyevski's *The Idiot* and forward in time to Kafka's short story about Gregor Samsa, 'Metamorphosis', that was later adapted, written and performed as a play by Berkoff. Both these works deal with similar political themes, those of oppression by those of higher social status and the struggle for survival of the worker. These are stories of disillusionment and loneliness.

Taking it further

One of the works left unfinished by Büchner at his death was *Lenz*, a prose work about *Stürm und Drang* writer Jakob Michael Reinhold Lenz.

When *Woyzeck* was first published

Woyzeck was first published as *Wozzeck* in 1878 by Karl Emil Franzos. Modernism was developing as a theatre form in Europe at the end of the 19th century, so it's hardly surprising that the text was rediscovered and reworked by Franzos at this time. It must have seemed to him to be very contemporary and highly appropriate for this moment. Modernism explored the inner psyche of the human being; writers had wanted to get inside the heads of their characters. Büchner challenges us to do just that with *Woyzeck;* we ask ourselves: what is wrong with the man?; why is everyone so cruel to him?; what's going on with the Doctor, asking him to only eat peas?

These changing styles brought more overt political messages to challenge audiences. There were performances of plays such as Ibsen's *A Doll's House* which exposed audiences to what life is really like, a life where there are no happy endings. Ibsen's plays involved a battle against idealism, and developed the work of The Moscow Arts Theatre. They showed how characters could be psychologically rounded and understood, as in real life.

When *Woyzeck* was first performed

There was a gap of more than 70 years between Büchner's death and the first performance of *Woyzeck* in 1913 in a now unified German nation. The early 20th century was a time of huge commercial expansion in German theatre: many theatres of varying kinds had opened offering a variety of experiences. Audiences wanted new and exciting experiences, and the idea of 'show business' took hold. In France, the **Café Concert** had become a huge theatrical industry, providing entertainment for the masses. Notions of censorship and taste were being challenged. The British **Music Hall** was another version of this.

Key terms

Café Concert
Music Hall

Many of the theatres of this period were sumptuously decorated buildings; others were much more basic. The Residenztheater in Munich where the first performance of *Woyzeck* took place was one such beautiful building, which had been built in 1750–1755 as part of a complex of royal buildings and decorated in rococo style. Theatres were owned by many different kinds of people, often professional actor managers who produced, sometimes directed and even starred in their own shows.

These were highly charged political times – the First World War would begin a year later and life across Europe would change forever. In the theatre, there was a tug-of-war between producers who wanted to retain the status quo of earlier, more formal and traditional theatre offerings, and those who wanted to push the boundaries of politically-based theatre. However, there were still the limitations of state censorship of live theatre.

Woyzeck hid its political ideas behind the façade of a simple story about an ordinary, if mentally unstable, man. The play would have been enjoyed by an audience, many of whom were unhappy with life in the land ruled by Kaiser Wilhelm, who was soon to go to war, then to abdicate as the country's ruler. At a time when the class system was soon to be turned on its head, the ideas and emotions explored in a play like *Woyzeck* would have been pertinent to its audience.

Performance history

The earliest performances

What was the style of acting like?	Naturalistic acting had already been developed by Stanislavski in Russia, but most acting was not in this style. Modernist theatre had challenged this in demanding less characterisation from actors. To our eyes these first performances of *Woyzeck* would probably look highly stylised and quite 'music hall' in nature. There were no microphones, so voices had to be very well developed. There are songs in the play and some of the performance would have been sung, with or without accompaniment.
What was the theatre like?	The theatre this play was first performed in was big, sumptuously decorated and very comfortable, particularly for those who could afford good seats. There was a proscenium stage and the audience were arranged in tiers, as in traditional London theatres.
What were rehearsals like?	Directors were generally part of the cast, often the actor manager of the theatre company. We do not know how long rehearsals took for *Woyzeck*, but companies were made up of actors who would have been familiar with each other and had worked together many times. The star system was well developed so the audience may have known the lead actors.
What do we know about the audiences?	Audiences were large; theatre was a very popular pastime. Many would have been the 'bourgeoisie' (people with money from the middle classes), while those in the cheaper seats would have been from all walks of life, including students. Ticket prices were highly competitive because there were so many theatres to choose from.

Structure, style and genre

Structure

Büchner intended the play to be disjointed and the writing suggests that each scene was to be played separately. This helps to explain why there has been so much debate about the order of the scenes. Some writers think that the play is like a series of images depicting the struggle of Woyzeck, each one building on the last to create the whole story. This was new to audiences when it was written, and even when it was first performed in 1913.

The play is made up of a series of short scenes which are similar in structure. Scenes begin with a character entering then moving the action along: in Scene 2, the Drum-Major enters, marching the length of the street; in Scene 3, Marie and Woyzeck enter during the singing. What does this mean? Does this make us sit up and take notice? This device makes the work very episodic, and makes us take a breath at the start of every scene. It is Büchner's way of calling us to attention.

The play is short and uncomplicated, with each scene forming a complete episode of action. This makes us work on the meaning after we have left the theatre, as we have to stick it all together in our minds. Some directors have said the play is like a series of pictures, strung together for us by the writer.

There have been many books written about the structure of this play, debating which version Büchner intended as the 'final' version. David G. Richards' book, *Georg Büchner's Woyzeck: A History of Its Criticism* (Boydell and Brewer, 2001), covers the continuous debate over the order of the scenes and the many theories that have been advanced since the writer's death.

Style

Defining the style of *Woyzeck* presents problems. The play has expressionist features, in that it explores the workings of the human psyche and how the natural world exposes characters to the horrors of life. However, it is interesting that Büchner wrote his play long before expressionism evolved: he was ahead of his time.

The play was written near to the end of the era of romanticism in Europe, and there are references to how Woyzeck is tossed about by the cruelty of natural forces, such as his growing madness. The play does invoke some sympathy in us for Woyzeck, but not in the way that *Camille* by Dumas, *fils* encourages us to empathise with someone. In this play, written in 1852, the lead character, a prostitute called Marguerite, commits the sin of falling in love with one of her clients and she dies. The play shows its audience a romanticised version of their own world, but then shocks them with its cruelty. The message is clear, and what the later practitioner Boal would term 'coercive'.

> **Key term**
>
> Greek tragedy

Some writers say that Woyzeck is like a character in a **Greek tragedy** who has no power over his own life and what he does. He lives in a mystical place that they describe as 'Elysian'; it is not real. He has to fight for his life. Woyzeck's survival, or otherwise, depends on the forces of nature. However, this is not a Greek tragedy. Woyzeck is not controlled by the actions of supernatural beings; he could exert self-control over his destiny, but he does not.

Key terms

alienated
fairytale
slapstick comedy
tragedy
epic theatre

Other writers think his story is being told by the Grandmother, with the Journeymen there to comment on the action, like a Greek chorus or like the Moon and the Woodcutters in Lorca's *Blood Wedding.* These characters lend the play a magical, mystical feel. They invite us to observe, just as Brecht does in *Mother Courage.* We feel separated from the action, or **alienated**, as Brecht would have us feel about drama.

The earlier *Stürm und Drang* writers thought life was a struggle to survive against the odds, contrived by nature's forces. Büchner was clearly influenced by these men.

Activity 1

Retell Woyzeck's story to another student, as accurately as you can from memory. What do you both feel about Woyzeck as a man? Can you decide why he seems to lose his sanity?

The language of the play is simple; some people thought it was crude when first performed. The language denotes the ordinariness of the characters. They are peasants and soldiers, apart from the Captain and the Doctor. The language is staccato when read aloud.

Activity 2

Stand facing your partner, at opposite ends of the studio. Try speaking the lines between the Captain and Woyzeck at the start of Scene 5, without the shaving.

a) How close do you think the characters have to be to each other, to make the best sense of this scene?

b) How urgent does this dialogue sound?

c) How can you play the scene close together with Woyzeck shaving the Captain, but still keep the distance in the relationship between the two characters?

d) Try to relate what you are doing to what you know about Brecht's work. Put in some of the dialogue to your story, share the exercise with your partner and tell it to a small audience.

Genre

To define the genre of *Woyzeck* is to take a bold stand! There are as many ideas about the genre of this play as there are drama critics. It is a play, maybe a tragedy, with some music. It is not a comedy, although it is funny at times.

Those who think the play is a story told by the Grandmother call it a 'black **fairytale**' that ends in Woyzeck killing himself out of total disillusionment with society. The characters show us how the writer is criticising society; they are almost caricatures, like characters in a fairytale. They are not fleshed out, but simply help Woyzeck to tell his own tale.

Taking it further

Think about the work of Steven Berkoff in *Metamorphosis* and compare it with that of Arthur Miller's *The Crucible*; one is seen as **epic theatre**, the other as naturalistic. The nature of the narrative in *Woyzeck* is similar to that of *The Crucible* – a lone man victimised by his situation and having the wrath of others piled on his head – but it is treated in a much more callous and impersonal way as Berkoff does in *Metamorphosis.* Can *Woyzeck* work if it is played naturalistically?

Activity 3

Try playing Scene 6 in a range of ways: fairytale, **slapstick comedy**, **tragedy**. How does using the main characteristics of a genre help you understand the play?

Research

Rehearsal techniques

In Section A of the exam, you will be asked to write about your ideas for rehearsals (with reference to a given extract from the play). Your techniques as a director will depend on the approach you are taking and your production concept. You may also have the approach of a particular practitioner in mind, and references you make to appropriate practitioners should enrich your answers.

> Use your knowledge of practitioners from the AS course to inform your responses and ideas here.

Acting style and practitioners

As director, you will have to make this fundamental decision of style before you approach the casting and rehearsing of this play. The most obvious choices include epic theatre, using the ideas of Brecht, and **physical theatre**, exploring the ideas of Berkoff and Théâtre de Complicité. Consider the three suggested approaches below.

> **Key term**
>
> physical theatre

The Brecht approach

- Actors will be cast in roles, but will also play minor characters. Ask the actors to work in pairs to produce an enacted summary of the action of the play, Woyzeck's personal experiences and the murder scene. This will inform the ways you go about directing the work, and help the actors get to grips with the scope of the narrative.

- Working with the actors playing Woyzeck and the Captain, ask them to perform Scene 5 with Woyzeck making his movements huge, then gradually diminishing them until you find the best way to inform the audience of how he feels about the other character. Ask the actor playing the Captain to address his lines directly to the audience, involving them in his performance as if it were a cabaret show.

- Working with Marie and Woyzeck, ask them to play the murder scene as if it were a boxing match. How does this influence what the audience thinks?

The Berkoff approach

- Ask the whole cast, who will be playing individual roles and minor parts as well, to devise an image that suggests a population repressed by authority and class. Use this as your opening tableau.

- Rehearse Scene 1 with Woyzeck and Andres behaving as if they are in danger (they have briefly escaped the drudgery of their normal lives), then go into Scene 2 with the actors as a struggling band of citizens in danger of being caught out by their oppressors. Words are snatched and urgent. This may help you create a sense of the oppressed as a desperate group, who are not necessarily looking out for one another.

- Bring in the Drum-Major; his presence alters the way the whole group behaves. Explore the physicality of Marie's behaviour and how it develops with the Drum-Major.

- Play Scene 15, creating a fight of extreme violence, watched by the whole cast. This will help the actors find out how their characters feel about Woyzeck. Is he worth saving? Is he just a madman, expendable because he is so difficult?

> **Tip**
>
> Directing stage fights is an expert process, so if you were going to explore this, you would need some help from a fight specialist. Professional theatre companies usually employ a fight director. You could explore the idea of interpreting the violence of a fight through tableaux and slow-motion methods such as Steven Berkoff often uses when he directs.

The Complicité approach

- Take Scene 3 and create a circus scene from the whole cast. Add a physical enactment of the astronomical horse and a monkey, and explore how the cast members create the scene while still coming into character to play their lines.

- Your work with the actors will involve a continuing flow of live pictures, created by the whole cast. The places and scenery for each moment will be suggested through physical movement and shape. Try out the murder scene with actors creating a moving scene of trees and water around Woyzeck and Marie.

Characters and relationships

If your work is going to have scenes of naturalism, you will need to explore the characters and their relationships, as they develop through the play.

- The actors playing Marie and Woyzeck should explore what it was that brought these characters together. This might have been physical attraction, Marie's need for support and Woyzeck's inability to survive on his own. Ask the actors to explore some of these ideas through improvised scenes of when they first met.

- Hot-seat the Captain to help the actor find out how powerful he really is.

- Ask all the actors to talk through times when they have felt overpowered by their situation, where they have not acted very well towards others to save their own skin. Use their body language to help you, as director, develop the physical performances of your cast. This is a psychological approach, as defined by Stanislavski.

- Ask your actors to explore how mental illness has been seen through the ages. Improvise scenes that highlight some of the most extreme examples.

- Play each scene with actors speaking their objectives, as they go, matching their movements to their objectives.

Remember that work you carried out for Units 1 and 2 could contribute here, particularly your preparation for your Unit 2 performance.

Voice

Your casting of your actors will have to take account of the vocal performances you want to achieve. You should cast performers with the clear capability to produce the voices you want. You will want to develop accents, tones and pace, according to your production.

Many directors use an accent or dialect coach so that the cast members develop their performances in an integrated way. For example, you may wish Drum-Major to speak with the voice of a British sergeant major: very loud, perhaps with a dialect such as cockney, and proud. You may wish the peasant cast to have a regional dialect and this will need to be tackled by yourself or a coach. You will need to help your actors produce the correct level of age, class and tone that suits your production.

There are songs in the play that will need to be vocally directed and, as director, you will decide on accompaniment or the lack of it. Tom Waits' version included some of his own compositions in his inimitable style. This production was highly expressionistic, using the kind of imagery associated with German theatre from the early 20th century and from silent films. His music was also highly Germanic, cabaret-style with a dissolute feel to it.

Many American, German and Danish productions have required the actors to overemphasise their speech, using the style of German expressionist theatre.

Movement and physical theatre

Depending on your choice of style, you will have to explore the way your actors will move around the space. If you are going for a physical theatre performance, you can use the ideas outlined in the 'Acting style and practitioners' section on page 109. Physical theatre performances generally enlarge and expose their characters through emphasised, and sometimes grotesque movement.

- Ask your actors to play a paired scene as if they had to communicate it to an audience a mile away. Bring the movement down in scale, and experiment with what this does to the meaning of a scene.

- Try out ways of walking for each of the characters. Ask each actor to walk as their character at five different times of their life. Each time, as director, add the idea that a major event has just happened to them.

If you are exploring the play through more naturalistic methods, your actors must find the ways their character moves by working in rehearsal very closely in character. For example:

- Woyzeck may have a limp or a facial tic, brought on by his poor condition. The actor must find ways of incorporating these into each scene, developing their intensity perhaps as the narrative progresses.

- Grandmother may need to bring out the grotesque characteristics of the play, or she might be an all-seeing witness to the events and be played as such.

- Ask all the cast to perform in character, as if they were animals. They have to decide which animals. Play some dialogue as animals, then ask the actors to reduce the exaggeration until you find the best level for each character. (This is a Maria Ouspenskaya activity; she was an early follower of Stanislavski.)

Text and sub-text

Your initial decisions about editing or not editing the text will determine your final version. After the initial read-through, many directors will work through the scenes in chronological order. Others will work on key scenes first. Some will run whole-cast workshops as a way of exploring the text with their cast. This gives you plenty to write about: what you are going to do with your actors, which exercises you will use in your explorations and the possible results of these.

You will have determined what you think is the sub-text of certain scenes before you start work with your cast, but much of this will also come through as you rehearse. It is important for a director to be flexible in rehearsal. For example, if the actor playing Marie does not know if Marie was actually a prostitute or not, she can play her scenes both ways, emphasising her motives and wishes. Working out some clear objectives for each character in each scene really helps actors with these problems.

Directing *Woyzeck*

There are all sorts of choices that you, as director, will have to make, but first you need to have a clear view of your own production, and this will involve some big decisions. Your process rehearsal will follow on logically from these big decisions. In your practical work on the text, you will be able to explore how your decisions will affect specific scenes and moments in the play. They will determine what kind of interpretation yours could be.

Style and genre

You may want to consider the style and genre of the play first. If you see the play as a comedy, your work as a director would involve working out how to make your audience smile and laugh. If you see it as a tragedy, you would need to focus on the obvious horror of the plight of Woyzeck, Marie and their child.

If you see it as a comedy	Read through the text and write down what you think is funny about the story. For example: • Woyzeck's relationship with the Doctor • The fact that Woyzeck can only eat peas for several months • The characters of the Drum-Major and the Sergeant • The Showman and the phenomenon of the astronomical horse • The relationship between the Captain and the Doctor. These all have comic possibilities. Try reading the lines aloud. Are they funny? Do your actors need to develop as caricatures and play larger than life in order to make them funny?
If you see it as a tragedy	Write a summary of what happens to Woyzeck and Marie, and then perform it. Try to determine why this happens to them. Is it their own fault? Who is responsible for Woyzeck and Marie's downfall? Is it because they are stupid? Is society fundamentally cruel to them? Is Woyzeck simply going mad? What is the clearest message of the play?
If you see it as a fairytale	What is magical about this play? What or who is the astronomical horse? Is the play an allegory told by Grandmother? If it is, what difference does this knowledge make as to how you are going to interpret the play? Are all the characters simply caricatures, created from a set of stock gestures, words and deeds? Try playing Woyzeck as one of the *commedia* caricatures, such as Zanni, a poor fellow from the country whose job it is to fetch and carry for others. He never makes his way. Marie could be played as Columbina, a country girl, often swayed by the affections of men; she is simple and easily distracted. What do you learn about the play by forgetting about character development, but instead concentrating on the messages in the play? This might focus on the good and evil in the play.

Taking it further

Commedia dell'arte is an ancient form of travelling improvisational theatre that originated in Italy in the late 16th century. This style of free popular theatre was concerned with ideas of love, adultery, jealousy and the desire to marry, among other subjects. The plots of each performance would often explore things going on at the time, exposing the antics of real people as they went about their business, much to the amusement of the audience. *Commedia* is still performed all over the world today.

Key term

commedia dell'arte

Character relationships

To explore the character relationships and help you develop your interpretation of the play, it is useful to make a list of the characters who have scenes in pairs and groups, and then do the activity below.

> ### Activity 4
>
> a) Taking the Woyzeck/Marie relationship, write down the things that each might find attractive about the other.
>
> b) Some writers say Marie is a prostitute. Do you agree? Is this a sexist viewpoint? Play a scene between Marie and Woyzeck as if she is a prostitute, and then as if she is not. When you decide on this aspect of Marie's character, you will have made a very important decision about the heart of this play.
>
> c) Explore the relationships of Woyzeck/the Doctor and Woyzeck/the Captain. These are fundamental to how your interpretation will unfold. You could try a simple status game: within each pair, determine who has a high status and who has a low one. Vary these status levels and decide which help you explore the characters more thoroughly.

Will you edit the text?

Since we do not know how the writer really intended his final version of the play to be, you might want to consider making some alterations to the version you are interpreting. Any director has this choice to make. To see if you do want to change the scene order, try some experiments:

Start your interpretation with the final scene when Andres discovers the blood in the woods, meets Grandmother and she goes off singing. This gives you the opportunity to use the idea that Grandmother is the storyteller. This device allows her to tell the audience the story.

This device might lead you towards the idea that Grandmother controls Woyzeck's life; he might then be played as a character in a fairytale, or as a clown caricature from *commedia*. The other roles in the play could be played by other clown caricatures. Your actors would then need to have time to explore this way of interpretation with you in the studio, and this would need to be allowed for in your production planning. This form of interpretation takes away the need to get inside the head of each character, as it is the storytelling that is important. Each character becomes a blank canvas on which the story unfolds.

Any director can edit lines out of a text, and some even put some in, but you cannot add in lines for this exam. If you want to create a shorter interpretation, you should always ask yourself how coherent the results will be. The play, as we have it, is quite short; it only runs for about 70 minutes.

Which stage form will you choose?

As this play is open to being interpreted in so many ways, you are completely open to interpret the text in any way you like, as long as your work would result in an integrated performance.

You might, for example, experiment with the physical theatre form and explore interpreting each line through movement, giving the meaning another dimension. To help with this, you could find out about the work of Théâtre de Complicité or Kneehigh, two companies that are renowned in this field.

> **Edexcel Examiner's tip**
>
> Tom Waits has written extra songs for his version. You can find information about this popular version on his website: http://www.tomwaitslibrary.com/woyzeck-main.html.

These companies explore texts through movement, creating meaning for the audience through physically creating the world of the play. They use the actors' bodies to make the scenery, the places, as well as the characters themselves.

Activity 5

a) Look at the circus scene with the astronomical horse. In a small group, explore ways of creating a horse figure that can move and speak, just like a horse might. Use this group as horse, as one character. Play the scene. Think about what this device might be for. For example, is Büchner commenting on the way society looked at uneducated humans, the peasants, treating them as sub-human?

b) Explore the idea of music as accompaniment to this scene, or all of them. There are some excellent film soundtracks that could prove suitable. Listening to Tom Waits' music for his production might give you some ideas.

Physical theatre companies often multi-role in their work (the cast list for the play suggests how you might do this). This means that the audience is less likely to feel the need to identify closely with a particular character; individual characterisation becomes less important to the actors as well. They all contribute to the making of meaning for the play as a story.

What will the stage area be like?

The space where you choose to mount your production will determine, to a great extent, how you are going to direct the script. The table below looks at three of the possibilities you might consider.

The proscenium stage	This is how *Woyzeck* was first performed. Performing within a fixed 'frame' creates a particular experience for your audience. It allows the audience to watch the action, to sit back and observe the life of the characters. Stanislavski thought that this allowed the actors to 'be' the characters they play, rather than just act them. If you decided on this staging and style, you would need to allow time for your cast to truly discover the characters within themselves. They would need to experiment, using their own particular emotional memories of things that have happened to them, and work out the objectives of their characters, as they progress through the narrative.
	This style often implies a need for scenery. How realistic do you want your set to be? Make a simple design of a set that can be easily developed, by adding or taking away elements. Your set might be fantastical, or have elements of realism in it.
	You may want to have no set at all; this might suit a space for a physical theatre adaptation or the epic theatre style. The ideas of Brecht will help you here, such as wanting the audience members to easily perceive the workings of the stage so that they never forget they are watching a play, not real life.
In-the-round	This style is commonly used in studio theatres. See page 150 of the AS Student Book for an explanation of what in-the-round can do for you as a director.
	Essentially it means there is no 'front', so the audience is drawn into the action. This might lead you towards working up the circus scene as a way into the play.
	This might then suggest circus-style music as accompaniment for your performance, dressing the whole cast as circus performers, multi-roling their way through the story.

Studio	This may well be the type of space you are most familiar with, as it is the most commonly used in student productions. Having your audience on one side or end allows you an identifiable space for the performers, makes lighting design relatively straightforward and provides a space in which almost any style of acting can take place. The intimacy of a studio means your audience gets close to the action and the actors, providing its members with a challenge, one that the play was always meant to deliver.

Design elements

The performance space and theatre form you choose, and your proposed budget will determine the design decisions you take.

The set

You may wish your production to have a full set, but then ask yourself how this relates to what Büchner tells us about the places where the action happens. There is no suggestion of reality in his writing, so a naturalistic set, full of props, would seem alien to this piece. However, there are defined locations, like a tent for the Showman, woods and water, which you will have to deal with. For example:

- The tent could be cloth presented by a group of actors, or simply a line of actors' arms and bodies, from which the Showman appears.

- The woods could be trees created on set from wood or lighting effects, or could be performers creating the shapes of trees.

- A range of levels could be created from blocks to give the performance space shape and some areas of different height, for example to give perceived status to characters such as the Drum-Major and the Captain. Blocks surrounding the acting area may provide the claustrophobia you want your audience to feel.

- You might set your action amongst your audience, to make the performance feel dangerous and unnerving.

- You may not wish to have any kind of set, providing an empty space for the performance to take place. Your actors create all the meaning for the audience through their performance alone.

Period or contemporary?

You might decide to update the play to the modern day, or set it in any other time in history. The crucial point is what you think changing the time will add to the meaning for your audience. The version you are using here is a modern translation of *Woyzeck,* so the language itself does not bind you in history. As the themes of the play are universal, you may think it does not matter when you set your play.

You might choose to:

- Leave it as it is. There is no reason that forces you to update any of it because the modern translation makes the language perfectly understandable to a contemporary audience.

- Move the action to the present day. The story is one of the everyman, struggling against class repression and casual cruelty, looking for love and understanding in a world he sees breaking down around him; he is battling with his own sanity to make sense of it all. Many contemporary dramas explore these themes.

Edexcel Examiner's tip

When students write about a performing space they have never experienced, their work sometimes lacks authenticity. For instance, you might suggest performing *Woyzeck* on the Olivier stage at the National Theatre in London. You may feel its huge revolving stage would be of enormous theatrical significance to your production. However, without some very thorough research into how a revolve of this capacity works, its pitfalls and safety regulations, your ideas may appear unconvincing. It is better to write things you are sure about, and always ask yourself whether your plans would be workable.

Taking it further

Steven Berkoff suggests in his play *Actor* that the more you bring onto the stage, the more the meaning of the text is weakened. His work is generally performed with the minimum of set and props.

- Choose a historical period in which to place the action. For example, your drama might take place in an occupied state, such as one of the old Eastern Bloc countries before the fall of the Berlin Wall, where free will has been sacrificed to a common external power, and where the common man is forced to rely on his wits to survive. Your work would need to use design elements, such as costume and props, to suggest a place and time; this may not be a real place, though, and it could be an imaginary occupation. The expressionistic qualities of Berkoff's *Metamorphosis* or *The Trial* (adaptations of stories by Kafka) could provide ideas for the context of your production here. The idea is that this is an undefined place of oppression where the world appears to conspire towards the downfall of the principal character.

Key moments

Working on key moments is an effective way of tackling a text. In any play, each director will consider different scenes which are pivotal to their interpretation.

How you open *Woyzeck* will be vital to which scenes you think are key. If you open with the text as it is written in the Edexcel version, Scene 1 will give your audience a chance to meet Woyzeck interacting with his friend Andres, showing how superstitious they are, how little formal education they have, and how connected they are to the natural world.

If you take the scenes in a different order, going back to the example of Grandmother telling us the story, your opening will be her lines in Scene 20. Then you must decide how to tell the story.

As director, you could take the following scenes, which cover the main aspects of the narrative, and pinpoint moments where action determines the outcome for the main characters:

- The opening
- The circus
- Marie's meeting with the Drum-Major and her betrayal of Woyzeck
- The Captain telling Woyzeck about Marie's meeting with the Drum-Major in Scene 9
- The murder of Marie.

Another approach would be to take scenes that expose the ways Woyzeck is used or betrayed by others. These could be:

- The opening
- Marie meeting the Drum-Major
- Scene 5 with the Captain
- Scene 8 with the Doctor
- The fight with the Drum-Major
- Grandmother's speech in Scene 20
- Scene 22 where Woyzeck is exposed as a murderer.

Your choice will be driven by the interpretation you wish to mount.

Interpretation

Woyzeck has continued to be performed over the years and it remains a popular choice for directors. The table below covers some of the more notable interpretations.

1913	The Residenztheater, Munich, on 8 November. First performance of *Woyzeck*
1914	The lights go out in theatres all over Germany and Europe as a result of the First World War
1925	First performance of the opera *Wozzeck* by Alban Berg at the Berlin State Opera
1979	Oscar-winning film version by Werner Herzog, starring Klaus Kinski as Woyzeck
1994	Film version by Hungarian director János Szász which transfers the action to twentieth-century Budapest
2000	*18 November,* Tom Waits and Robert Wilson's musical version opened in Copenhagen. The dialogue was first in Danish, with songs in English. It was later translated to English, performed 2002

Ultimately, a production of *Woyzeck* should resonate with modern audiences because of its universal story of the everyman fighting with the powers of oppression that he sees around him. He struggles to maintain a relationship with a partner because he cannot see another way to live a successful and happy life. This is a world where civilisation is a very thin layer hiding the baser instincts of man – surely something that surfaces throughout theatre history, in contemporary drama and in many aspects of modern life.

Further reading

Benn, M., *The Drama of Revolt: A Critical Study of Georg Büchner (Anglica Germanica Series 2).* Cambridge University Press, 1979.

Keith-Smith, B., *Büchner in Britain: A Passport to Georg Büchner.* Mellen Press, 1987.

Leacroft, R., *The Development of the English Playhouse. An Illustrated Survey of Theatre Building in England from Medieval to Modern Times.* Cassell, 1988.

Richards, D.G., *Georg Büchner's Woyzeck: A History of its Criticism.* Boydell and Brewer, 2001.

Russell-Brown, J., *The Oxford Illustrated History of Theatre.* Oxford University Press, 1995..

Styan, J.L., *Modern Drama in Theory and Practice: Realism and Naturalism.* Cambridge University Press, 1981.

Styan, J.L., *The English Stage, a History of Drama and Performance.* Cambridge University Press, 2008.

Wallis, M., and Shepherd, S., *Studying Plays.* Arnold, 1998.

Useful websites

http://www.tomwaitslibrary.com/woyzeck-main.html
Tom Waits' website has a range of articles, clips and reviews of his production in 2000, including lyrics to some of his songs, composed for the production. Waits' CD *Blood Money* (Epitaph/ ANTI, 2002) has his songs for the play.

EXAMZONE

This written exam is worth 30% of the available marks for your A Level course and it is therefore important that you prepare for the paper as thoroughly as possible. You will be under exam conditions for 2 hours and 30 minutes, during which time you have to answer three questions, two on the chosen text (the first of which is divided into three smaller parts) and one on the play that you have seen in performance (see page 70 for a breakdown). This is the only time on the A Level course that you will be required to work under written exam conditions, and it is a good idea to start to prepare for this as early as possible in the A2 year so that you will gain as many marks as possible in this paper.

When looking ahead to Unit 4, it is worth looking back at the AS course and reminding yourself about what has gone before and the demands of the written elements of the two units. During the AS year, you were required to write the following:

- Exploration Notes (up to 3,000 words)
- Evaluation of a live theatre performance (up to 1,000 words)
- A rationale/concept for Section A of Unit 2 (up to 500 words)
- If applicable, a rationale/concept for Section B of Unit 2 (up to 500 words).

All of these will have been prepared under supervised or controlled conditions which, although not exactly the same as exam conditions, will have given you some indication of how to complete work on your own from prepared notes. There will have been opportunities in Unit 1, for example, to discuss and evaluate aspects of the chosen texts in relation to the elements before you compiled your own set of notes in response to practical exploration of the chosen texts. This experience has a direct bearing on your work in preparing for Unit 4 and it might be worth having a look at a sample set of Exploration Notes to remind you of the elements that were explored and the kind of information you drew from that experience. Preparing for Sections A and B of Unit 4 will be very similar and make the same sort of demands on you.

The live theatre evaluation that was also an important part of Unit 1 is worth considering in relation to the general demands of Section C of Unit 4. Although there is more to the question in the written paper than there was in Unit 1, the basic response to the live production as a member of an audience will be very similar.

You need to draw upon the performance values that you recognised in Unit 1 to help you structure an approach to your notes for Unit 4 and answer the question.

The rationale/concept you wrote in the preparation for your performance in Section A of Unit 2 is a response to the chosen monologue or duologue, or design element, and indicates your understanding of your chosen skill in the context of the play. This experience will be valuable when preparing the text for Sections A and B. You will probably have kept a working notebook of the preparation process, putting the role into the context of the play as a whole. The notebook may help you when it comes to defining an approach to the Unit 4 text that a director might adopt in order to bring out what you might consider to be its essential themes for a 21st-century audience.

EXAMZONE

By referring back to experiences to date, you can focus on the demands of Unit 4 in relation to what you have already been involved in when looking at writing about drama and theatre. You have probably already built up a substantial bank of useful words and phrases that you will be able to draw upon when considering the written exam.

Unit 3 also has a written element that requires you to compile a Supporting Written Evidence document in relation to your experience of devised theatre for performance. This, too, should help you to focus on terminology, practitioners, and structuring concise responses to a range of given demands. There is a suggested format to the written element of Unit 3 in the specification, with a list of areas that might be covered in your document. This information, together with the information on the AS year, should help you when it comes to looking at Unit 4 as there is nothing here that you should not be considering when preparing the Section A and B text in your role as director.

You will be able to access a wider range of marks in Unit 4 if you go into the exam with the confidence of knowing that you are able to structure sentences and paragraphs that reflect your understanding of the drama experience. The paper is about you and your understanding, but it is also about showing an examiner that you have understood and are able to use a developing range of drama terminology to effectively express your ideas on paper in response to the focus questions. There is a skill in writing under exam conditions in response to a question, and you need to be aware of the demands of the unit as early as possible in the A2 year in order to help you to prepare in a structured way.

You must take your annotated copy of the chosen text into the exam with you to help you answer the questions in Sections A and B. You and your teacher must decide how much annotation there needs to be in your text. In the exam itself, you will not have time to read copious amounts of notes to help you to access the questions, so if there is too much, this is almost as unhelpful as if there is not enough. Striking a balance is very important, and to help you do this you need to remind yourself that:

• Section A is about you as director planning a rehearsal for a given extract from the chosen text

• Section B is about you as director planning for a performance of the chosen text for a 21st-century audience.

Your annotation therefore needs to inform your responses to both these sections. It might be that you have a particular approach to your annotation that makes it easier for you to access the information quickly under exam conditions.

If your script is A4 size, with blank pages on the left as you open it up, then you might use the left-hand pages for your director's concept, and the pages containing the body of the text itself on the right-hand side for your rehearsal ideas. You will know when you open your script in the exam room that information for Section A is on the right-hand side, and information for Section B is on the left.

E X A M Z O N E

Whilst there may be some overlap of information, you will be able to focus more effectively than if you are having to skip through a number of pages in order to gather one set of thoughts.

Any annotation should be in response to practical activity around the chosen text. You are not allowed to take any pre-published material into the exam. This might include:

- Theatre programmes
- Extracts from books/magazines
- Downloads
- Pictures or photographs stuck into your script.

Your version of the script is only helpful to you if you have prepared it with the questions in mind. Your script might contain the following:

- A family tree of the central characters and their relationship(s) with other characters in the play
- A brief plot summary
- A drawing/sketch of your set/staging that you could copy into your answer booklet, probably in response to a Section B question, if appropriate
- Drawing/sketches of costumes for central characters that you can copy into your answer booklet, probably in response to a Section B question, if appropriate
- A key inside the front cover of where to find particular scenes/important moments that you might want to draw upon to support your response to either question. Whilst you must respond to Section A in relation to the extract that you will be given in the exam, you may have other sections of the text that you have annotated with particular rehearsal techniques and strategies that you could apply equally as well to the given extract. Section B is about bringing your interpretation to life for your audience, but you cannot write about the whole play in this response as there will not be time; you may have some key moments of the text in mind that you can draw upon, as appropriate, to support your answer.
- Passages of the text annotated in relation to rehearsal techniques or strategies that you have used to explore those extracts in practical workshop activities.
- Passages of the text highlighted with more detail written on the left-hand page to support your overall director's concept/interpretation of the text to bring it to life for your audience.

Section A

Section A is about you as director responding to the given extract as if you are planning a rehearsal. The question is about your approach to the extract and you are not required to make connections with other sections of the text. The section is worth 20 marks out of a total of 80 available marks for the unit. It may be the case that you consider the allocation of marks and decide to spend 30 minutes on this section, leaving 60 minutes each on Sections B and C.

EXAMZONE

You will need to plan your approach carefully, particularly as this section has a question that is divided into three parts, each of which has a different focus in relation to preparing the extract for rehearsal.

You need to remember that there are no right or wrong answers here; the question is about you and what you would do in relation to what the questions are asking.

Your response does need to make sense in relation to how you might approach rehearsing the extract, and whether or not the rehearsal methods or strategies you describe would be appropriate to the chosen text. This is something that you will have explored in workshops before you do the written exam, and your annotated script should contain ideas for rehearsals that would be appropriate and relevant.

The breakdown of marks available in this section gives you some indication of how much information is required. Question a) has 4 marks allocated, b) has 6 and c) has 10. Clearly, more information is required for c) than for a). You need to look at the Sample Assessment Material produced by the exam board and see how much space has been given to each question in the sample answer booklet. Whilst there may be some adjustment to this in the answer booklets available from 2010, the basic principle is the same, and you need to structure your response in relation to the amount of space you have been allowed and the mark allocated for each part of Section A.

Section B

Section B is about you as director responding to a focus question in relation to your proposed concept for the play in performance. There is a choice of question here, and you should look carefully at what is demanded from each question before deciding which of the two you are going to respond to. There are no right or wrong answers here, but do make sure you are addressing the demands of the question, not simply describing your concept to the examiner. It is not difficult to lose focus in a written exam, particularly in the extended responses of Sections B and C, so it is always worth looking back at the question at the end of each paragraph to see how effectively you have responded to it before moving on to the next paragraph.

If you are asked to 'outline and justify your approach to a production of the play staged in your chosen performance space', then you need to be very clear what the question is looking for.

The starting point of your response here is 'outline and justify'. The word 'justify' is the one that your examiner will be looking for in relation to the mark scheme, and how successful your response is at meeting the criteria. Without justification of your ideas, your response may not gain more than Level 3 which is worth between 13 and 18 marks out of 30.

Before going into the exam, you need to have an annotated copy of your script that will remind you of your approaches to the following elements that a director needs to consider for a performance:

E X A M Z O N E

- Social, cultural and historical connections to the original performance conditions of the play
- Design elements and how they connect and combine in your overall concept
- Specific moments/highlights to be expanded on in answers where appropriate to do so
- An overall concept/interpretation as your response to the original, and why you have chosen to approach a production of the play in the way you have.

Your examiner is looking for a structured response to the question, giving clear examples of how your performance might work for your audience in the chosen space, and justifying decisions you have made. The use of appropriate terminology will be taken into account in the marking, along with the quality of your written communication, which includes clarity of expression, the structure and presentation of ideas and grammar, punctuation and spelling. This will be more evident in the longer answers – Sections B and C and probably part c) of Section A.

The examiner is not looking to question your directorial decisions as long as they make sense in relation to:

- the original intentions of the playwright
- the chosen question
- the theatre of the 21st century and what is possible in live performance.

Whatever your concept is, you need to be able to justify it in terms of how an audience might have reacted to the original performance of the play, and what you feel you need to do to it in order to engage your 21st-century audience. This kind of question asks you to be very specific in your response, and to focus on the performance space. Other types of question could look at one or more design elements, or your approach to exploring a particular character or group of characters in your interpretation. Whatever the focus of the question, remember that you need to support your decisions if you are looking to achieve marks in Level 5, which is the top band of marks.

In order to prepare for Section B, you need to have the mark scheme enlarged and visible to you when looking at preparing answers. Look at the space in the answer booklet and think about the expectation that you will be able to fill this space with relative ease in the exam. You will only be able to do this if you regularly practise structuring responses to the kind of questions you are likely to be asked in the exam. You need to accept that there will never be a question in this unit that simply asks you to 'tell us about' or to 'describe' what you would do to bring the chosen text to life for your actors and for your audience. Everything that you consider putting into your answer booklet needs to be supported by reasons: 'this is what I would do, and this is why I would do it' or 'this is what I think, and this is why I think it'.

Everything that informs your response to Section B should come from your understanding of the chosen text, coupled with your understanding of how theatre works in performance. This knowledge will have been gained during all aspects of the course to date, and the more live theatre you can see, the more you will be able to draw from that experience in putting together your own ideas for performance.

SECTION C

In Section C you are required to:

- see a live performance of a play written and performed in a specified period

- study and research the original performance conditions of that play

- evaluate the ways in which directors, designers and performers have used the medium of drama to interpret the play in the contemporary performance

- compare the production you have seen with how the play would have been performed in its original time period.

You will study one of the following three broad periods of theatre history:

1. **525BC–AD65:** This takes in the period of classical Greek and Roman tragedies and comedies, which is seen as providing the foundation of modern Western drama.

2. **1564–1720:** This period (starting with the birth of both Shakespeare and Marlowe) takes in the extraordinary explosion of drama in the Elizabethan and Jacobean periods, as well as the changes after the Restoration of Charles II to the throne following the closure of theatres under Oliver Cromwell.

3. **1828–1914:** Starting in Büchner's lifetime and finishing at the beginning of the First World War, this period takes in the late Romantic movement, the rise of melodrama and the development of realism and naturalism.

> Each of the three plays which are possible choices for your Section A and B answers fits into one of these periods (1. *Lysistrata*; 2. *Doctor Faustus*; 3. *Woyzeck*). For Section C, the period you write about must not be the period your play for Sections A and B comes from. For example, if you study *Doctor Faustus* in Sections A and B, then you must not write about 1564–1720 in Section C. This means that you will broaden your knowledge about drama and theatre.

In each of these periods, major developments in drama and theatre took place, and a wide range of plays were written and performed. You will develop an informed overview of one of these periods, and understand the original performance conditions of the play which you will see in a live production.

The exam

You are allowed to take your research notes on the play you have seen into the exam. These notes can include drawings, sketches and diagrams, but no pre-published material (from books or websites). Your research notes for Section C must not be more than 1,000 words in length. More guidance on Section C in the exam is given on pages 153–155.

Original performance conditions

When researching the original performance conditions in relation to your chosen play, you will be considering:

- the nature of the playing space (the theatre), its shape, size and physical characteristics

- the nature of the audience and the relationship between the actors and the audience

- the technical features of the theatre: the ability to deal with set, lighting, sound and special effects

- the playing conventions and acting styles which are enabled by the conditions (for example, asides; naturalistic performances)

- any economic factors that play a part, for example in the attitude to costume, make-up, props and set.

In the pages that follow, these factors are considered in more detail for each of the specified time periods.

525BC–AD65

Areas to consider

In this part of the exam, you will be asked to think about the approach taken by a modern director and actors in a production of a play first performed over 2,000 years ago. You will need to know what theatres were like then, and what performance techniques were used, as well as understanding something of the historical and social context in which your chosen play was written. This will help you to think about the approach taken to the same text by a modern theatre company.

Then and now: to what extent do the social, cultural and historical conditions surrounding the creation of the original work impact on a modern day production of the play?	The performance space	How does the theatre architecture differ in scale and shape? Where are the entrances and exits in relation to the original? What is the effect of a space designed for open air performances compared with that of an indoor space? What features of the original performance spaces are carried through to a modern production?
	Theatre technology	How are lighting and sound used? What similarities and differences are there in the use of scenic devices (e.g. trucks, painted flats, curtains, flying, raised areas, three-dimensional and two dimensional scenic structures)?
	Performance factors	The festival and competitive nature of Greek theatre. Drama and its relationship to other forms of entertainment. The length and time of performances.
	The audience	Who went to the theatre in ancient Greek and Roman times? What size was the audience? Which elements of society attended performances?
	Actors and acting styles	How were actors thought of at this time? What is the effect of performing in masks? How many were in the Chorus? To what extent is the acting style naturalistic?
	Actor-audience relationship	What was the relationship between the actors and the audience? What was the effect of using the orchestra compared to the *logeion* (Greek) or *pulpitum* (Roman)? To what extent were the audience addressed directly?
	Themes and ideas	How do the themes of the plays reflect the concerns of the society of the day? What do they say about how far Man has control over his own destiny? What do the comedies say about the politicians and politics of the day? How have the themes and issues been emphasized and made relevant to a contemporary audience?
	The text	Who has translated or adapted the play? How does it compare to other versions? How literal or free a translation is it? How does the use of language compare to the original (e.g. use of verse).

This period of theatre history begins with the birth of the Greek tragic playwright Aeschylus (c. 525–c. 455BC) and ends with the death of the Roman tragic playwright Seneca (c. 4BC–AD65). This period marks the beginning of theatre in the Western world. It brought about the emergence of the playwright, the development of buildings in which plays were performed and the establishment of acting as a means of artistic expression.

The words 'drama' and 'theatre' are derived from Greek words, the former meaning 'action' and the latter having its origins in 'theatron', the place where an audience sat to watch a performance. There is no way of telling how the rituals associated with the agricultural calendar were transformed into the more sophisticated art form of theatre, but at some point in the 6th century BC these acts of worship became a form of storytelling. The theatre buildings that developed, first as wooden structures, then built of stone, were based around natural slopes on a hillside leading down to a flat circular space.

Epidaurus Theatre, Greece

Timeline

550BC	500BC	450BC	400BC	350BC	300BC	250BC	200BC	150BC	100BC	50BC	AD50
534 Establishment of dramatic festivals at Athens	496 Sophocles born; Pratinas of Philus writes first Satyr play	448 Aristophanes born	384 Aristotle born	350 Theatre built at Epidaurus	291 Menander dies	240 Romans import Greek model of theatre; Play by Livius Andronicus performed in Rome	195 Terence born	130 Pacuvius dies	86 Accius dies	25 Vitruvius writes De Architectura with plans for theatre buildings	AD 2 Use of front curtain suspended overhead
524 Aeschylus born	484 Euripides born	431 Peloponnesian War begins	380 Aristophanes dies	342 Menander born	270 Naevius born	239 Ennius born	184 Plautus dies		75 First stone-built theatre at Pompeii	5 Seneca born	AD 65 Seneca dies
508 Democracy begins in Athens	472 Aeschylus introduces second actor	411 Aristophanes writes Lysistrata	380 Plato's Symposium	335 Aristotle's Poetics	254 Roman Plautus born	220 Pacuvius born	170 Accius born		70 First amphitheatre at Pompeii		
500 Theatre of Dionysus remodelled after the collapse of wooden seats	468 Sophocles attributed with introduction of third actor	406 Sophocles and Euripides die		329 Circus Maximus in Rome, appearance of clowns and flute players		219 Caecilius Status born	169/8 Ennius and Caecilius Status die		55 Theatre of Pompey built in Rome		
	456 Aeschylus dies	404 Athens defeated in Peloponnesian War		322 Aristotle dies		201 Naevius dies	160 Terence dies				

NB: These dates are approximate, as our knowledge of the period is quite fragmentary and it is virtually impossible to be precise, so there may be some variance with other sources.

The origins of Greek drama

As part of the ritual to honour the god Dionysus, the god of wine, youth and fertility, a hymn known as the *dithyramb* was sung and danced by a chorus of around fifty performers. Since song and dance do not rely on literacy, they came before the drama. The actor, playwright and possibly priest, Thespis (from whom we derive the word **thespian**), is credited with being the first person to have a character stepping outside of the chorus and having a solo role, and we know that he won the first contest of the City Dionysia festival in 534BC.

The main evidence we have about Greek theatre is almost entirely derived from the theorist and critic, Aristotle (c. 384–c. 322BC) and the surviving plays of five dramatists:

Tragic: Aeschylus (c. 525–c. 455BC); Sophocles (c. 496–c. 406BC) and Euripides (c. 480–c. 406BC)

Comic: Aristophanes (c. 448–380BC) and Menander (c. 342–c. 291BC).

Key term

thespian

The other sources of information are records of the festivals, images from Greek vases and mosaics, and the architectural remains of the theatre buildings such as those of the Theatre of Dionysus in Athens and at Epidaurus.

In the late 6th century BC, the ruler, Peisistratus, authorised a competition of tragic plays that ended with a **satyr play** as part of the spring festival in honour of Dionysus. Three other dramatists from this early period are known to us: Choerilus (writer of over 150 plays and an innovator in the use of costumes and masks); Pratinas (who is thought to have invented the satyr play) and Phrynichus (who is believed to have introduced female characters and written about issues of the day). Sadly, none of the works from this period have been found, which is why our knowledge of Greek plays starts with Aeschylus' *The Persians* (472BC), the earliest surviving play.

The origins of Roman drama

Roman theatre is often described as a poor imitation of Greek theatre, largely due to the fact that the Romans conquered Greece around 146BC and took much of its culture. Until around 240BC, Roman theatre was more about entertainment than drama and was a place to see jugglers, acrobats, trained animals and sporting events such as chariot races. As the Romans began to invade Greek territories, they began to imitate and translate Greek plays. The comedies of Plautus (c. 254–c. 184BC) and Terence (c. 195–c. 160BC) were highly popular in their day and are the only surviving examples of Roman drama from this early period. One of the significant differences between Roman and Greek comedy is the absence of the Chorus and the introduction of five or more characters. Shakespeare's *The Comedy of Errors*, for example, is based on *The Brothers Menaechmus* by Plautus, which has a cast of ten.

The tragedies of Ennius (c. 239–c. 169BC), Pacuvius (c. 220–c. 130BC) and Accius (c. 170–c. 86BC) appear to have been mostly Roman adaptations of Greek originals, but only their titles and fragments of them remain. From the later period, nine tragedies by Seneca have survived and they are all based on Greek originals. There is much debate about whether Seneca's plays were actually performed or whether they were just written to be read. Whatever the case, Seneca's plays were a major influence on **English Renaissance** tragedy in their depiction of violence (Seneca's version of *Oedipus*, for example, has Jocasta ripping open her womb on stage), and in their use of a five 'act' structure.

The Romans altered existing Greek theatres and changed the auditorium into a semi-circular shape, but within the city of Rome itself, temporary wooden structures were used until around 55BC, when the first permanent theatre was built. Roman theatres were more enclosed and included a raised stage (the *pulpitum)*, a much smaller *orchestra* area and a building across the back of the stage (the *frons scaenae)* with ornate columns and entrance doors.

Alongside tragedy and comedy, the Romans developed **farce** and **mime**, which were non-literary entertainments until around 100BC. The writers Pomponius and Novius began to write lines of dialogue for what had been a largely improvised form of theatre, and they created afterpieces to follow the main drama, similar to that of the Greek satyr play. What is interesting about these is that they featured four stock characters: Bucco (a braggart); Pappus (a comic old man); Maccus (a fool and a glutton) and Dossenus (a grotesque hunchback), who are thought to be forerunners of the types found in *commedia dell'arte* which developed some 600 years later.

Comparisons and connections

In Section C of the exam you are asked to make informed judgements about a contemporary performance of a Greek or Roman play, and make comparisons with its original performance conditions. You are more likely to see a modern production of a Greek play than you are a Roman play, because more Greek plays have survived and there are far more contemporary productions of Greek plays each year in English than there are Roman. You are not required to judge a modern production on how closely it resembles the original, as there are numerous ways of tackling the different aspects of the original production; you are simply required to make a comparison.

As well as focusing on the conventions and treatment of the drama by a contemporary director, you need to consider how these might differ from the original staging and performance conditions. The notes you produce to help you answer the exam question need to draw upon your reaction to the live performance seen and the research information you have collected on the historical context of the play. You are likely to be asked to focus *either* on the production elements of a performance and the way it has been staged, *or* on the acting aspects of a production and the methods and techniques that have been used by the actors.

The performance space

> **Tip**
>
> Look closely at the illustrations in this section. Use your imagination to explore what it would be like to be on that stage, and in the audience.

The original performance space for a Greek tragedy or comedy was virtually in-the-round with the audience banked up, looking down on the actors. There was a building known as the *skene* facing the audience, one side of which acted as a façade. In the later period there was a raised platform (the *logeion*) running across the back of the circular performing space (the *orchestra*) with an entrance door or doors (*thyromata*) at the back. Above the 'stage' was some sort of hoist or crane known as the *deus ex machina* from which a god could be lowered at the end of a play, usually to sort out some complication in the plot. The most important thing to remember about the Greek theatre is the scale of the space, which was more like a modern sports stadium than an enclosed theatre space (see photo page 125).

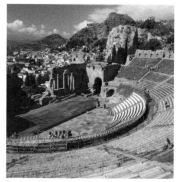

Roman Theatre in Sicily

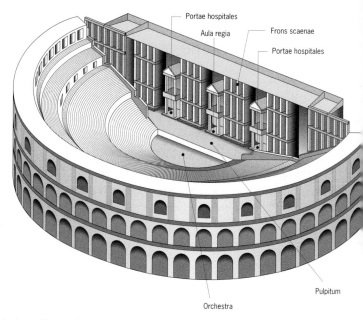

Portae hospitales

Aula regia

Frons scaenae

Portae hospitales

Pulpitum

Orchestra

The Romans adapted the Greek outdoor theatre spaces and developed buildings of their own on a similar scale, with a seating capacity of at least 5,000. The most significant difference between Greek and Roman theatre spaces is the way in which the Romans altered the shape of the orchestra from circular to semi-circular. This had the effect of bringing the stage (*pulpitum)* and the back wall of the stage (*frons scaenae*) closer to the audience. The Romans added up to five doors in the *frons scaenae* to represent the entrances to houses. The central door (the *valva regia* or *aula regia*) was for the principal actor and the most important character in the play, the doors on either side (the *portae hospitales*) were for the characters next in order of importance, and the outer doors (*the itinera versurarum*) were for the lower order characters. Having characters running in and out of doors is an important ingredient of the plot in the comedies of Plautus, and has continued to be a comic device throughout the history of drama (see reference to farce on page 126).

Scenic elements

Beyond the architectural elements of the theatre buildings themselves, it is difficult to assess the extent to which the Greeks or the Romans used scenery. In the 2nd century BC, the Greeks added painted scenery to the front of the *logeion*; this was known as the *proskenion* (meaning in front of the *skene*) from which we get the modern term **proscenium**. The Romans painted the *frons scaenae*, but this was probably part of the fabric of the building rather than something designed specifically for the play being performed. The Greeks used a wheeled platform called an *ekkyklema* which may have been used to reveal a tragic scene that occurred off stage, such as Medea slaying her children. The modern equivalent of the *ekkyklema* is a **truck** which may have been thrust out from the central opening doors. Some scholars think that it was just used to present a **tableau**, but whatever its original purpose, it is a useful scenic device that you may find in a modern production.

The Romans introduced the use of curtains (*aulae*) which were placed at the front of the stage and decorated to act as a backdrop to the play being performed. They also used smaller curtains (*siparia*) on stage to disguise a character or scenery that might appear later in the play. It may have its origins in later Greek theatre, but the Romans also created the *periaktos* – a large three-sided prism which has a different location painted on each face. The prism rotates on a central axis (or on a wheeled turntable) so that the relevant painted face is towards the audience. There was one on each side of the stage and this was later increased to three. Later versions known as *telari* had removable panels so that more than three locations could be indicated. The *periaktos* is still used today as a way of representing quick changes of scenery.

Key terms

proscenium
truck
tableau

Costumes

When plays from this period were originally staged, the actors probably wore everyday contemporary clothes. When you see a modern production of a classical play, ask yourself to what extent the costumes suggest ancient Greece or Rome. Servants and lower order characters are likely to have worn drab clothes made from cheap material, whereas the higher order characters would be dressed in more colourful garments made from finer fabrics. Does the costume design reflect the social status of the characters, and how has this been achieved in the contemporary production?

Masks

The wearing of masks was an essential element of performance in ancient drama. For tragedy, Greek actors wore the *onkos,* which was elongated in shape with a large headpiece. Refer back to the more detailed description of masks on page 84.

An actor wearing a mask cannot perform in a naturalistic style. Masked performance requires stylised gestures, controlled movement and a heightened awareness of the way the voice projects and communicates through a mouthpiece. The mask subsumes the actor, who has to inhabit it and project a role from behind it. The choice to use masks or not in the production of an ancient text is a major directorial decision and will impact on the performance style of the production.

Music

We know that whole sections of Greek plays were written to be sung, but we have no way of knowing what music from this period sounded like. In ancient Greece and Rome, the most prominent instruments were the stringed **lyre** (and a larger version of it known as the *kithara*) and an early version of the flute. Scholars believe that music, song and dance in this period were inextricably linked. The Greek and Roman armies used trumpet-like instruments and these may have found their way into the theatre. Music is an essential element in theatre of this period, and a director has to decide on the form that it takes in a contemporary production. Be prepared to comment on the instrumentation used, the singing style adopted and the overall dramatic impact of the music in the performance you see.

Key term

lyre

The Chorus

The first decision a director has to make is how large to make the Chorus. The early Greek plays may have used a Chorus of 50, but this is reduced to 24 by the time of Aristophanes. By the time of Plautus, the Chorus is a single performer who has the function of a narrator or prologue. The economics of a contemporary production and the use of smaller performance spaces often mean that the Chorus in a modern production is in single figures. Having decided the scale of the Chorus, the next issue is how to use it on stage. The ancient practice was to keep the Chorus on stage once they had entered, and for any mask or costume changes to happen on stage. How, when and where the Chorus enters and exits is something to look out for when you are watching a live performance.

There may be an attempt to have a unified Chorus so that they look and sound the same, or alternatively, each member may be given an individual identity and personality. The dialogue or poetry may be spoken in unison, or it may be divided up between individuals or groups, and you need to be aware of the effect this has on communicating meaning to the audience. Some or all of the Chorus sections may be sung rather than spoken, and this will add a musical dimension to the presentation of these parts of the production. The use of masks, costumes, and grouping and positioning around the set are all decisions that have to be made in relation to the Chorus. How the Chorus looks, sounds and moves will affect the overall style of the production. Look back at the information on the structure of *Lysistrata* (page 79) and the handling of the Chorus (page 84).

Sound and light

These are two theatrical elements that are available to the modern director that were not in use in the theatre of 525BC to AD65. There may have been some primitive use of sound effects, but this would have been limited to the banging of wood or metal. All performances were staged in the afternoon, with the possibility of using lighted torches and fires towards sunset. Creating the time of day or night or an interior or exterior location was not a practical option as it is in a contemporary production. Look at how a modern production uses stage lighting and recorded sound.

Gods, myths and religion

For the Greeks and the Romans, the destiny of humans was controlled by a host of deities led by Zeus, in the case of the Greeks, and Jupiter, in the case of the Romans. The theatre was, in effect, part of a religious ritual, and plays were performed in honour of the gods. The role of the playwright was to question and explore the relationship between humans and the gods. The majority of tragedies from the period retell ancient myths (largely based on Homer) where the hero is pitted against the will of a god or gods. This tension between the rational (the human) and irrational (the divine) is a fundamental issue that a modern director has to address, and you should be able to comment upon how this theme has been treated in the production you are reviewing.

Working on the text

It is important that you get to know about the play before seeing the performance. Even if the translation or adaptation you are going to see performed is different to the one that you study in class, the basic outline of the plot and the characters will be more or less the same. (see p132) In some ways it is useful to study a different version, as it gives you a useful benchmark with which to compare the live production. Noticing differences and similarities between texts provides you with a useful starting point for both your discussion work in class and in your production notes.

Activity 1

Create a storyboard of the play. Look at each scene and summarise it in as few words as possible. Just try to say who is in the scene and what happens to them. You can either draw a cartoon to depict the scene or take a digital image by setting up a still image with others in your group. Write a caption summing up what happens in the scene and add speech balloons to the characters saying something key to the scene. Try to capture the whole plot of the play in a series of pictures on one side of A4 or A3 paper. This will help you retain a visual memory of what happens in the play before you go and see a performance of it.

Activity 2

Here are some practical activities for working on the text:

a) Choose a central scene and act it out first without wearing a mask and then wearing one. How do the performances differ? How does your relationship with the other actors change? What is your relationship with the mask? How does it affect the delivery of lines? What does this tell you about what to look out for when you observe a masked or unmasked performance of an ancient Greek or Roman play?

b) Experiencing an ancient theatre space. Whilst there are no Greek theatres in the UK, the design of the Olivier Theatre in London's National Theatre is based on the Greek Theatre at Epidaurus and is worth a visit. The remains of nineteen Roman amphitheatres exist in Britain. Visiting one will give you some sense of scale. Failing that, find a hillside with a hollow the size of a football pitch at the bottom of it and you have something approximating the size of a Greek or Roman amphitheatre. Once you have found the space, try acting out a scene with other actors in the space. What does it tell you about the acting style required?

c) Create a modern version of a scene from the play using today's language. How well does it work? What are the differences?

d) Restricting the space. Use a 20–30 metre length of rope that makes a square, rectangle or circle. Members of the group create a 2-3 metres square or diameter performance space by holding the rope up and out. Act out the scene, making it as emotionally truthful as possible. Try to keep it small, like a performance for television. Then gradually extend the rope until the performance space is as large as the room (or even better as large as an outside space). As the performing area becomes bigger, the performers should make their performances larger and louder without losing the emotional truth.

e) Take it in turns to direct each other in a scene, exploring different objectives of the characters or intentions of the scene.

f) Investigate the prop and costume requirements of the play. For example, there may be a requirement for armour and swords or for an actor to enter wearing a huge phallus strapped to their waist. See how they affect the movement of characters on stage and the other characters' reactions to you.

Preparing for the live production

Your appreciation of a production will be greatly enhanced if you read the play before you see it. Most classical Greek and Roman plays are available in Penguin Classics editions (www.penguinclassics.co.uk). The version of the play you see may not be available in print, but having an idea of its content and structure will give you a reference point from which to consider how the director has altered and interpreted the original. Reading the play will help to familiarise you with the often unusual names of characters and places.

Try and get to your seat at least 20 minutes before the performance begins. This will give you an opportunity to look at the set in some detail. It is a good idea to draw a sketch of the performance space, and note the use of levels, colours and textures.

Research and production notes

The notes you take into the exam room will help you to:

• recall your response to the live performance

• record the results of your research into relevant theatre history.

The following table may help you to organise your thinking and the knowledge you have gained about the original performance conditions from your additional research.

Production aspect	Now	Then
Treatment of themes (including the gods) • In a tragedy, how are the gods and the religious elements treated? • In a comedy, how are the satire and political elements approached? Have changes been made to ensure it has contemporary relevance?		
Performance space • How close is the audience to the performers? How does this affect your experience of the play? • Is there a use of space and levels that emulates the *orchestra/logeion* of Greek theatre or the *orchestra/pulpitum* of Roman theatre?		
Scenic elements • Are any scenic elements such as *ekkyklema*, *deus ex machina*, *periaktos* or *aulaeum* used?		
Costume • What are the costumes like? How do they differentiate between characters? What period and/or style do they create?		
Masks • Are masks used? To what extent are they authentic or contemporary?		
Music • How and when is music used? As accompaniment? To create atmosphere? As underscoring? What is the instrumentation? Is it recorded or played live?		
Chorus • How is the Chorus used? How many are there? Are they masked? How are they moving? Are they singing? How are they positioned within the space?		
Sound and light • How are sound and light used in the production? How effective are they and do they add significantly to the effect of the performance?		
Acting style(s) • How would you describe the way the actors are performing? Is it declamatory? Stylised? Are there elements of naturalism to the acting? • How are the actors speaking and moving?		

Before the visit

This is a key moment in your course and you want to make the most of it. It may be helpful to refer back to pages 67–75 of the AS Student Book for general advice on the evaluation of a live performance. This will remind you of areas to consider.

It's a good idea to reread the text slowly, remembering all the work you've done on it. Check through your notes, flagging up key points for yourself about the original staging.

Research the theatre where the performance is taking place. Most theatres will have photographs on their websites, or online booking diagrams showing the shape of the theatre and auditorium. Research the company which is staging the play. Are they well known for any particular style or approach to texts from earlier periods? Look at their marketing and publicity material; does it tell you what their approach will be?

During the performance

When you go into the theatre, compare it with the theatre in which your play was originally staged. Look at the table on page 132. You may find it helpful to take a copy of it with you as a checklist. Make some initial notes before the play starts about the audience, theatre and acting area. Get a programme and read the notes it if you have time. If not, read them later.

Give yourself time to make notes at the interval and the end. Reflect on your images of the original production, and note areas of contrast. Try to spot if cuts or alterations have been made to the text. One obvious area of difference will be the use of stage technology. Note how lights, sound, projection and special effects are used, and how effective they are. Do they add significantly to the effect of the performance? If so, how?

Note down all the thoughts you have had. Discuss the play with others, but don't lose your own impressions. Make more notes when you get home, or the following morning. Look again at the programme. It may contain an interview with the director outlining his intentions, or references to earlier productions, for example.

Preparing for the exam

You are not allowed any pre-published material in the exam, only your own notes. These may be up to 1,000 words, but may also include drawings, sketches and diagrams. You should include visual information where relevant, for example sketches of the original playing space and the one you saw used in performance. Your notes should focus on the comparisons and contrasts which you have observed. It is helpful to include key terms (for example, 'proscenium'), ensuring that they are correctly spelt.

In the exam

Read the question, and think about it. You know that it will be focusing on the contrast between *then* and *now*, but what specifically is it asking you? Is the focus on the acting? The direction? The stage technology? The design? Make notes about the relevant areas. Put these in order as your plan of your answer. Write a brief introduction and then the main part of your answer. Read it through, and then write a brief conclusion. Read it through again.

Further reading

You'll find more detailed background information on Ancient Greek Theatre in the following books:
Beacham, *R.C.*, *The Roman Theatre and its Audience*. Routledge, 1991.
Easterling, P. and Hall, E. eds., *Greek and Roman Actors: Aspects of an Ancient Profession*. Cambridge University, Press 2002.
McDonald, M. and Walton, J., eds, *Cambridge Companion to Greek and Roman Theatre*. Cambridge University Press, 2007.
Wiles, D., *Greek Theatre Performance: an introduction*. Cambridge University Press, 2000.

Useful websites:
http://www.theatron.org
http://www.greektheatre.gr

1564–1720

For the exam, you need to think about how a modern director and theatre company have approached a play first produced about 300–450 years ago. You need to know about the original theatre conditions, as well as the social, cultural and historical background of your chosen text. You will then be able to form opinions about the choices made by a modern theatre company in the production you see.

Areas to consider

Social, cultural and historical elements provide the background to everything.	Theatre playing space	What were the shapes and sizes of performance spaces? Entrances and exits; built-in features such as balconies, trapdoors; structural features such as pillars. Roofed or unroofed?
	Theatre technology	Provision for scenery, furniture, props, curtains; lighting and sound, including music; special effects; scene changes; potential for 'flying' scenery/actors.
	Performance factors	Timing of performances; admission prices; geographical position of theatre; audience capacity; divisions inside the auditorium.
	The audience	How varied? Which social classes attended? How did they behave? What were their expectations? What were the main beliefs and ideas they held?
	Actors and acting styles	What were the predominant styles? How did actors achieve both physical and psychological approaches? Were there 'stars'?
	Actor-audience relationship	Physical relationship: how close was the audience? Did actors play to the audience? Did they involve them and improvise for them? Or not acknowledge them?
	Themes and ideas	Plays reflect important social and cultural ideas: kingship, religion, marriage, love, punishment and reward, for example. Different periods and societies have different main concerns, but they can also have a lot in common: why else would Shakespeare have more than a merely historical interest? Shared concerns also enable us to transpose settings to other times.
	The text	Are there different versions? Does the language present difficulties? Are there topical references that no longer mean anything to a contemporary audience? Will this make cuts/changes/adaptations more likely?

Then and now

So how does a modern director approach plays from this period? The first thing is to understand the period itself. It spans over 150 years, which means that it contains many changes and developments. Thinking about how much things have changed in this country in the last 150 years gives you some idea. There are the changes in technology such as radio, TV, mobile phones and MP3 players, as well as the invention of cars and aeroplanes. There are huge events such as wars, accidents and natural disasters. There are social changes, for example in education, healthcare, attitudes to sex or to 'green' issues. Although written by individuals, plays are products of the society of their time; modern directors need to make them work for the society of our own time.

It isn't possible in this section to give all the information relevant to all plays of this period. You will need to identify the areas relating to your particular play (and production) which will need additional research.

Background information

Time period	Monarch (name/ description of period)	Historical event	Theatrical event
1533–1603	Elizabeth I (Elizabethan)	1581: By this year, Elizabeth I had achieved a complete prohibition on the cycles of 'mystery' plays performed outdoors, seen as leftovers of Roman Catholicism.	1564: Shakespeare and Marlowe born 1576: The Theatre (first purpose-built theatre) is built in Shoreditch, London. 1576: First Blackfriars Theatre (indoors) is adapted for use from rooms in an old monastery. Used by 'The Children of the Chapel' (i.e. schoolboys) for performances. 1577 onwards: Several 'unroofed' theatres are opened: The Curtain, The Globe, The Rose, The Swan, The Hope and The Fortune are amongst these.
1603–1625	James I (Jacobean – from *Jacobus*, the Latin word for James)	1603: Queen Elizabeth I dies; Elizabethan period ends and the Jacobean period begins with the accession of James I of England to the throne.	1608: Shakespeare's company, the King's Men, starts using the Second Blackfriars Theatre as their indoor base. 1616: Shakespeare dies.
1625–1649	Charles I who was beheaded in 1649 (Caroline – from *Carolus*, the Latin word for Charles)	1625: King James I dies; the Caroline period begins with the accession to the throne of King Charles I. 1649: King Charles I is beheaded.	1642: Oliver Cromwell, the Lord Protector, who has taken power from the King, closes all the theatres in the country. Theatre buildings are broken up and public performances are banned by law.
1649–1660	No monarch: Oliver Cromwell was 'Lord Protector' until his death in 1658. (Period is described as 'The Commonwealth'. All public theatres closed from 1642–1660.)	1660: King Charles II (son of King Charles I) is crowned king; this is known as The Restoration (i.e. the restoring of the king to the throne).	In the world of theatre, the period of Restoration comedy is usually considered to be 1660–1720.
1660–1685	Charles II. (Period is described as 'The Restoration'. The period of 'Restoration Theatre' is usually taken to be 1660–1720, although style changed within this period.)	1665: The Great Plague of London. 1666: The Great Fire of London.	1660 onwards: Theatre performances become legal again. Various buildings (including covered tennis courts) are adapted to become theatres. 1674: The Royal Theatre, Drury Lane, a purpose-built theatre, opens. This signals the beginning of large-scale indoor theatres.

Three main types of theatre

Theatres and audiences changed during this period. There are three main types of theatre to consider. Although every theatre was individually designed, theatres shared certain features. Here are some examples.

1. The Elizabethan/Jacobean playhouse (1576–1642)

The Swan, 1594

Labels on illustration: Winch room, Gallery, Trap door, Thrust stage, Audience surrounding the stage, Yard, Groundlings stood here

Main features
The building and stage: theatres like this had a raised and flat **thrust stage**, which jutted out into the auditorium inside an unroofed, many-sided building (the effect was of a circle). There were two entrances at stage level, with a balcony at the back of the stage. There was a trapdoor entrance from the area below the stage. A sloping roof above the upstage area of the stage enclosed a winch room from which scenery and actors could be lowered. This was supported by two large onstage pillars. The acting area was large – about 14 metres wide by 9.5 metres deep at The Swan. Lighting was provided by daylight, but this could be supplemented with candles and burning torches. Sound effects were created live (thunder by rolling cannonballs down wooden chutes, for example). Music was live and could be played on stage, behind stage, below stage or on the **gallery**. Special effects could include fireworks of various types.

Theatres were built outside the city limits where restricting laws did not apply; they were often close to brothels and shared space with more basic entertainment such as bear-baiting. Performances typically started at about 2 p.m. A theatre like The Swan could accommodate an audience of about 3,000.

The audience: the basic entrance fee was 1d (one old penny) which was about the same cost as a loaf of bread (much cheaper than going to the theatre today). However, this only entitled you to stand in the area around the stage (the yard). It is therefore likely that the 'groundlings' were the poorest, least educated and rowdiest element in the audience. By paying 2d you could get a seat in the first tier; a further 1d took you to the next tier. A special box, which was named 'My Lord's Room' and placed centrally in a raised position, was available for patrons or dignitaries. Although the very poorest in London society were excluded by being unable to afford the entrance fee, and the very richest did not come as they could invite the players to perform in their own houses, a wide section of society was represented at performances.

Actors: each company was likely to have its 'star' actors, including comedians ('clowns'). Generally, the acting style would have been 'large', with speeches being recited with extended physical gestures. Naturalistic acting as we understand it was unknown. Soliloquies were shared with the audience, and the clowns 'played off' the audience, often improvising around the text. As actors and audience shared the same light and both were visible to each other, the performance felt more like a shared event. All actors were men, and female roles were given to boys.

Well-known plays written for this kind of theatre include: most of both Shakespeare's and Marlowe's plays; Kyd: *The Spanish Tragedy*; Webster: *The White Devil*, *The Duchess of Malfi*; Middleton: *A Chaste Maid in Cheapside*; Dekker: *The Shoemaker's Holiday*.

Taking it further

Visits to modern theatres which are built on the pattern of theatres from this period will be useful. Shakespeare's Globe Theatre on London's South Bank and the Rose Theatre in Kingston-upon-Thames (built in the shape of the Elizabethan Rose Theatre) are obvious examples. There are at least 12 replicas of the former around the world. Visit http://shakespeare.palomar.edu/theatre.htm for a virtual tour of one replica theatre.

The closeness of the actors to the audience in the modern Shakespeare's Globe Theatre

2. The Elizabethan/Jacobean indoors theatre

It's difficult to give precise dates for this type of theatre, as these included the halls in the houses of the aristocracy.

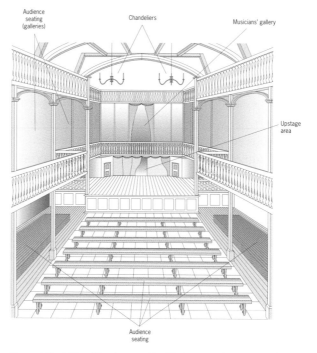

Audience seating (galleries) — Chandeliers — Musicians' gallery — Upstage area — Audience seating

Second Blackfriars Theatre, used by Shakespeare's company from 1608

Main features

The building and stage: theatres like this were 'private' or 'indoors'. They were smaller and rectangular (the building was about 30 metres by 15 metres). The acting area was about 20 metres by 14 metres. The entire audience was seated on benches, either facing the stage or in the galleries. They viewed the action from fewer angles than in the public theatres. There were no columns to interfere with sightlines. This progressively allowed for more stage illusion and effects, resulting eventually in 'masques' which were spectacular shows, with music, poetry and elaborate scenery and costumes. (Some masques cost the modern equivalent of more than a million pounds for a single performance.) Some natural light was available, but artificial light predominated with the use of candles and burning torches. One innovation was that music was played *between* the acts of plays, with the musicians in sight of the audience in the gallery behind the stage. The auditorium could seat 600 to 700 – about a quarter of the audience in a public theatre.

The audience: this was more socially select. It cost at least 6d to enter. The effect was to exclude the poorer members of society and create an audience of more privileged and better-educated theatregoers. They were likely to be less noisy and participative than audience members in the public theatres.

The actors: the same actors worked in both public and private theatres, but the nature of the audience and the indoor playing conditions probably meant that their acting style could be less broad and voluble, and the comedians were less vulgar.

Well-known plays written for this kind of theatre include: Shakespeare: *The Tempest*; Beaumont: *The Knight of the Burning Pestle*; Jonson: *Volpone, Every Man in His Humour, Bartholomew Fair, The Alchemist*; Marston: *The Malcontent*.

3. The Restoration playhouses (from 1660 onwards)

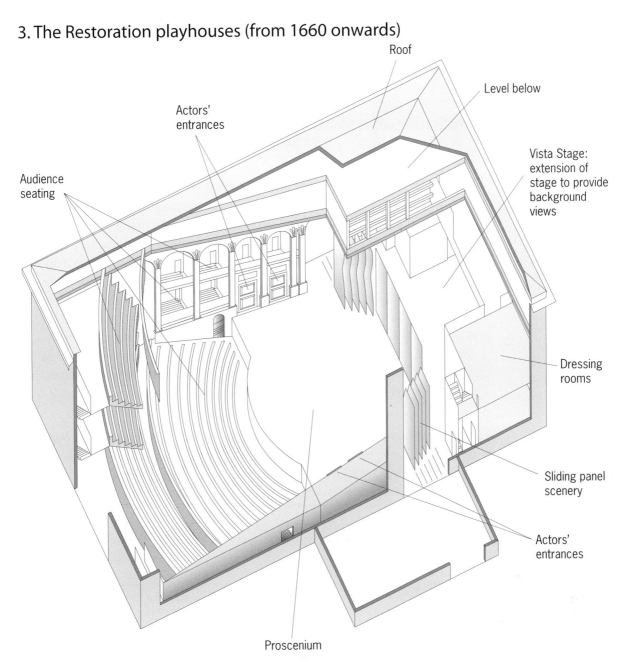

Roof

Level below

Vista Stage: extension of stage to provide background views

Actors' entrances

Audience seating

Dressing rooms

Sliding panel scenery

Actors' entrances

Proscenium

Theatre Royal, Drury Lane, 1674 (designed by Sir Christopher Wren)

Main features

The building and stage: this was developed from the indoors private theatres, rather than the unroofed Elizabethan public theatres. The building was rectangular and the majority of the audience faced the stage. All the audience was seated in a large pit, or in galleries. There was a picture frame (proscenium arch), but also a large proscenium stage (a forestage). There were sophisticated arrangements for moving scenery (four sets of grooves for scenery to be slid on and off) and a **vista stage** beyond this for additional visual effects. Artificial lighting was provided by suspended chandeliers, and both audience and actors were lit by these. **Footlights** made an appearance. Sound was still created live by stagehands. The theatre had become more visual, with scenery playing a more important part. The playing space was 14 metres wide and 9.1 metres deep. The auditorium held about 2,000 people, but the distances between actor and audience were on average greater than in previous theatres.

Key terms

vista stage
footlights

The audience: the cheapest seats were in the Upper Gallery, furthest from the stage, reversing the situation in the Elizabethan public theatres. These cost one shilling (12 old pence). The most expensive 'box' seats cost 5 shillings and seats in the **pit** cost 3 shillings. A small number of the audience could pay to sit on the stage. Theatre-going was becoming a middle- and upper-class pastime, although servants and other 'ordinary' people still attended. The audience could be badly behaved, however; there was a lot of rowdiness, and fights sometimes broke out.

The actors: the main innovation of the Restoration theatre was the introduction of actresses for the first time. This had a profound effect on playwrights and audiences; theatre became a very 'sexy' experience, and many of the plays of the time explore themes relating to sex, love, marriage and adultery. Roles known as **'breeches parts'** were written specially to allow actresses to display their legs. Actresses were often regarded as immoral. Many of the comedies reflected the society of the audience (in contrast to the classical drama and Elizabethan dramas which had previously been most popular), so it was important for actors to be able to imitate the sophisticated social manners required in movement and speaking. In theatres of this size, the acting style was necessarily large. The lighting remained dim, so there was an emphasis on physicality and gestures as well.

Well-known plays written for this kind of theatre include: Congreve: *Way of the World*, *Love for Love*; Wycherley: *The Country Wife*, *The Plain Dealer*; Aphra Behn: *The Rover*; Farquhar: *The Recruiting Officer*; Vanbrugh: *The Provoked Wife*, *The Relapse*; Goldsmith: *She Stoops to Conquer*; Sheridan: *The Rivals*, *The School for Scandal*.

Working on the text

As you work on the text you have chosen, you will divide your activities between practical work in the studio and research in the library and on the internet. This is how you will get to know the text really well. It is most important that you find out how to bring the play alive, as a piece of performance, because this is what the examination is asking you to write about.

Activity 1

Use your imagination to create a picture of what it would have been like to act your chosen text in its original theatre with the original audience. Imagine waiting in the dressing room (the tiring-house, as it was called then) and hearing the audience. What are you wearing? What props are you carrying? Imagine your entrance. What do you see and hear (and smell)? How does the audience react to your character and scene?

Activity 2

Here are some practical activities using the text:

a) Choose a key scene and act it out. Become familiar with the language and experiment with different ways of using and delivering it.

b) Create a modern version of the scene using today's language. How well does it work? What are the differences?

c) Act out the scene making it as emotionally truthful as possible. Try to keep it small, like a performance for television. Then gradually make it larger and louder, trying to fill a large space, without losing the emotional truth.

d) Perform the scene entirely in movement, ensuring that your gestures and moves express your character's feelings clearly and as fully as possible. Then act out the scene again, this time using the text.

e) Take it in turns to direct each other in a scene, exploring different objectives or balances in the relationship.

f) Try to set up the performance conditions of the original production. (To do so completely is impossible, but you should try to get a feel for what it was like for actors and audiences at the time.) Mark out the size and the positions of features of the stage and the position of the audience. Get the feel of entrances and exits (e.g. trapdoor, balcony).

g) Act out a scene in the space, and see how it is possible to use the distance between characters, or their positions on stage, to alter their feelings and the interpretation of the scene.

h) Get hold of some pieces of costume, e.g. rehearsal skirts, hats, formal jackets, boots, etc. which correspond to the theatrical costume of the period. See how this affects the formality of your movement on stage. (This can be applied to props as well, especially 'costume' props, like snuffboxes, fans and swords.)

i) Try playing comic scenes with an audience which participates (i.e. other members of your group). Place 'audience' members in positions they would occupy in the original theatre. What effect does this have on how you play the scene?

j) Experiment with the 'rhythm' of scene changes. (Relate this to the original playing conditions.) What is the effect of having one scene follow another very quickly (i.e. with the second group of actors coming on while the first group are still making their exit)? What is gained?

Preparing for the live production

This is a key moment in your course and you want to make the most of it. It may be helpful to refer back to pages 67–79 of the AS Student Book for general advice on the evaluation of a live performance. This will remind you of areas to consider.

Before the visit

Re-read the version of the play you have been working on or, if available, the translation you are going to see performed. Also remind yourself of moments to look out for that may connect to the original staging (e.g. the use of central doors). Find out about the theatre company that is performing the play or the previous work of the creative team (the director and designer) as this will give you some insight into their working methods. Research the theatre or venue where you are going to see the performance. Most theatres have a website containing a seating plan and possibly photographs of past productions that will help you visualise the shape and size of the space.

When you go into the theatre, compare it with the theatre in which your play was originally staged. Look at the table on page 134. You may find it helpful to take a copy of it with you as a checklist. Make some initial notes before the play starts about the audience, theatre and acting area. Get a programme and read the notes if you have time. If not, read them later.

During the performance

Use the interval (if there is one) and the time after the performance to note down your initial impressions of the production. Addressing the following five key points will give you a framework to expand your thinking later:

- How did the production use the space compared with the original staging conditions?

- What struck you most about the interpretation of the play?

- In what ways was the text different or similar to the one you have been working with?

- What technologies were used to create the visual impact of the production?

- To what extent did the production enhance or detract from your understanding and appreciation of the play and its original performance conditions?

Note down as many thoughts as you can remember about the production. Discuss the play with others, but don't lose your own impressions. Make more notes when you get home, or the following morning. Look again at the programme. It may contain an interview with the director outlining his/her intentions, or references to earlier productions, for example. Read any reviews of the production that may have been published and compare the critic's opinion with your own.

Preparing for the exam

You are not allowed any pre-published material in the exam, only your own notes. These may be up to 1,000 words, but may also include drawings, sketches and diagrams. You should include visual information where relevant, for example sketches of the original playing space and the one you saw used in performance. Your notes should focus on the comparisons and contrasts which you have observed. It is helpful to include key terms (for example, 'ekkyklema'), ensuring that they are correctly spelt.

Read the question, and think about it. You know that it will be focusing on the contrast between *then* and *now*, but what specifically is it asking you? Is the focus on the acting? The direction? The stage technology? The design? Make notes about the relevant areas. Put these in order as your plan of your answer. Write a brief introduction and then the main part of your answer. Read it through, and then write a brief conclusion. Read it through again.

Further reading

You'll find more detailed background information on Marlowe in the following books:
Bevington, D., and Rasmussen, E., eds., *The Revels Plays: Doctor Faustus*, A- and B-Texts (1604, 1616). Manchester University Press, 1993.
Cheney, P., ed., *The Cambridge Companion to Christopher Marlowe*. Cambridge University Press, 2004.
Gill, R., ed., *Doctor Faustus*. A & C Black, 2003.
Hopkins, L., *Christopher Marlowe: Renaissance Dramatist*. Edinburgh University Press, 2008.
Jump, J., ed., *Marlowe: Doctor Faustus*. Palgrave Macmillan Casebook, 1969.
Mangan, M., *Doctor Faustus*. Penguin Critical Studies, 1989.
Oz, A., ed., *New Casebooks: Marlowe*. Palgrave Macmillan, 2004.
Riggs, D., *The World of Christopher Marlowe*. Faber and Faber, 2004.
Simkin, S., *Marlowe*. Longman Preface Books, 2000.
Useful website:
http://www.theatron.org

1828–1914

For the exam, you are asked to answer a question that uses your understanding of theatre and performance during the years 1828–1914. You will need to apply this understanding to your modern experience of watching a play written in this period.

The live production of your chosen play is your 'primary source' for your research and exploration. This means that you must make sure you experience a production that fires your imagination and interest, both in the play and its performance history. You will need to form clear opinions about how the director, designers and performers involved in that modern production, have used the whole medium of drama and theatre to create what you have seen.

In addition, you need to understand what was going on in the world of theatre, and in the world itself, during the period in which your play was first written and performed. These make the social, cultural and historical background to the play. When you have a feel for the times, you can begin to understand what playwrights had to say to their audiences. Historical information helps you to place your own ideas in the original context of the first performances.

Areas to consider

Social, cultural and historical elements provide the background to everything.	Theatre playing space	This period covers the development of what we might call modern theatre. Almost everything we experience today in theatre began then. What were the shapes and sizes of performance spaces? Entrances and exits; built-in features such as balconies, trapdoors; structural features such as pillars. Roofed or unroofed?
	Theatre technology	Provision for scenery, furniture, props, curtains; lighting and sound, including music; special effects; scene changes; potential for 'flying' scenery/actors.
	Performance factors	Timing of performances; admission prices; geographical position of theatre; audience capacity; divisions inside the auditorium.
	The audience	How varied? Which social classes attended? How did they behave? What were their expectations? What were the main beliefs and ideas they held?
	Actors and acting styles	What were the predominant styles? How did actors achieve both physical and psychological approaches? Were there 'stars'?
	Actor-audience relationship	Physical relationship: how close was the audience? Did actors play to the audience? Did they involve them and improvise for them? Or not acknowledge them?
	Themes and ideas	Plays reflect important social and cultural ideas: kingship, religion, marriage, love, punishment and reward, for example. Different periods and societies have different main concerns. This period was one of huge social change and society's concerns were shifting.
	The text	Are there different versions? Does the language present difficulties? Are there topical references that no longer mean anything to a contemporary audience? Will this make cuts/changes/adaptations more likely?

This time period covers most of the Industrial Revolution in Europe, periods of massive social upheaval. There were 148 revolutions all over Europe, The American Civil War, The Franco-Prussian Wars, The Boer War, the rise of the Suffragette movement, and major developments in understanding science and the natural world.

Here are some of the main historical events that took place and that influenced playwrights of the day, along with some of the social developments that are related to them:

Time period	Location	Historical event	Theatrical event
1830	UK	The opening of the Liverpool to Manchester Railway, the start of the railway age: leads to social mobility.	*Black-Ey'd Susan* by Douglas Jerrold performed in London.
1832	UK	The Great Reform Act, the start of universal suffrage in Britain: broadens the electorate.	
1837	UK		Building of the Almeida Theatre, London.
1847	UK		The birth of the actress Ellen Terry. Performance of *The String of Pearls* by George Dibden Pitt.
1848	UK	Karl Marx publishes *The Communist Manifesto*, a basis for social revolution.	
1850	UK		Writing and first performance of Ibsen's second play *The Burial Mound*.
1855	India	The Indian Mutiny: increases desire for independence in the British Empire.	
1856	Russia	The Crimean War: leads to reform of medical care.	
1859	UK	Darwin publishes *On the Origin of Species*: challenges all religious faiths.	
1861–1865	USA	The American Civil War: leads to the establishment of a superpower.	
1861–1865	UK		Performances of *The Streets of London* by Dion Boucicault. The building of Theatre Royal Nottingham (1865).
1870	France and Germany	The Franco-Prussian War and the establishment of a unified Germany: changes the political map in Europe.	
1887	Russia		Chekhov commissioned to write the play *Ivanov*; he finishes it in two weeks.
1888	Sweden		Strindberg writes *Miss Julie*.
1898	Russia		Moscow Art Theatre formally set up (10th April).
1895	UK		Oscar Wilde writes *The Importance of Being Earnest*.
1898	Russia		Stanislavski directs Chekhov's play, *The Seagull*.
1899	South Africa	Boer War: questions the Victorian view of Empire.	
1903	USA	First aircraft flight: leads to new forms of transport and warfare.	
1913	UK		George Bernard Shaw writes *Pygmalion*.
1914	Serbia	Archduke Franz Ferdinand assassinated, the start of the Second World War: leads to 'the lamps going out all over Europe', C.G. Gray, Foreign Secretary, UK.	

The theatre itself

In this period theatre became firmly established as an indoor pastime. It was a hugely popular place to go, and what was on there catered for most of society.

By the early 19th century, the idea of a standing space for an audience, where mostly men assembled to watch and make witty ripostes to the actors on stage, was going out of fashion. Theatre managements made it their business to attract the ever-growing middle classes and artisans back to their spaces. They remodelled their theatres to provide more comfortable seating; instead of hard benches, or nothing at all, they put in stalls seats, which could be numbered individually, and sold in a more organised way. Seats tended to be upholstered and covered in velvet and velour cloth, and there was usually fitted carpet to walk on; thus audiences experienced greater comfort. The surroundings became reminiscent of people's own homes – at least those of the middle and upper classes. Managers installed lamps and covered the walls with pictures, murals and hangings.

This 'gentrifying' of theatre buildings resulted in better behaviour from their audiences. Being in a smart place often has the effect of calming people down, and can even make them rather in awe of the whole proceedings. Audiences were no longer able to shout out and throw things at the actors during the performance. Where the stage was set with furniture and often crockery and glasses, audiences were encouraged even more to behave as if they were in their own homes.

The wealthiest, most expensively dressed people occupied the orchestra seats at the front (the 'cheap seats' were at the back), and performers could communicate both subtly and overtly with them. In music hall performances, jokes and songs full of innuendo and smut might be directed to the folk with less sensitive tastes at the back of the auditorium, over the heads of the gentry.

The more expansive and emotional **melodramas** that had been popular up to this period began to be replaced with work that was more naturalistic, and that is one of the directions that theatre began to go in.

The shape of the theatre

Visual and aural elements

Almost all theatres were tall, solidly constructed buildings. The Almeida Theatre in London, for example, was first built in 1837 as a music hall where variety acts would perform as they toured the circuits around the country. The Theatre Royal in Nottingham was built for £15,000 in 1865 and took only six months to build. It had Corinthian columns and a classical façade. The Theatre Royal in Drury Lane, London, had been rebuilt in 1812 by Benjamin Wyatt after Sir Christopher Wren's theatre had burnt down, and it is still standing today. During the 19th century it was chiefly famous for its extravagant pantomimes.

Most theatres were designed with proscenium arch stages – the performing space was framed by the arch, like a picture frame. There were high spaces above the stage called the flies, used to hang curtains, tabs and scenery that could be dropped down on pulleys and ropes to the stage. They also allowed actors to be suspended on wires and 'flown' across the stage. Sets were developed in the 'box' style, where scenery surrounded the actors on three sides.

Taking it further

These major events had an effect on the ways playwrights thought and wrote about their world, and influenced what audiences wanted to see at the theatre. How people viewed themselves in relation to empire, politics and social mobility were reflected in plays of the time. Despite being very different plays, Chekhov's *The Cherry Orchard* and Wilde's *The Importance of Being Earnest* are both about social class, power and mobility.

Key term

melodrama

Key term

raked
backdrop

There was high **raked** seating, stalls, circles and galleries, rising upwards to the back of the theatre auditorium. Theatres were lit with candles, oil lamps and eventually gas lanterns and electricity. This was often dangerous and explains why so many theatres burnt down. There was no sound equipment so actors' voices had to be well developed.

This design of theatre still exists today, particularly in cities and big towns such as Bristol, Brighton, Manchester and London. Whilst what we see performed in modern theatres may be different, the shape and structure of the 19th- and early 20th-century theatres still influence the ways in which pieces are performed.

Ornate hand-painted **backdrops** and scenery were used to depict places and to simply decorate. We still see this kind of design in some contemporary productions.

Props and furniture became more and more important as the 19th century went on, reaching a peak in the work of Konstantin Stanislavski in Moscow. He believed that his sets should truly represent the physical context of the play. This highly ornate aspect of theatre design and set decoration is not seen so much today; generally furniture is simple, easily moved on and off stage and often transforming into different objects between scenes.

Who owned the theatres?

The 19th and early 20th centuries saw the growth of the 'actor managers' – these were performers who made enough money to own and run their own establishments. Here is an interesting example of the way this phenomenon worked:

In the county of Surrey in southeast England, standing near Westminster Bridge on Blackfriars Road, there was a theatre called the Surrey Theatre. In 1829 a play called *Black-Ey'd Susan* by Douglas Jerrold opened to an audience of people employed locally and for the most part on the River Thames. In this area the naval press gangs still abducted men to serve on ships, and this play dealt with that theme. The play elicits sympathy for the naval ratings, rather than the officers. The fact that this theatre attracted mainly working-class audiences meant that both audience and play were well matched.

About 40 years later, at a theatre north of the River Thames, a play called *Caste* was performed. In this play there is a naval officer as the hero, and a drunken manual labourer called Eccles who is greedy, stupid and incapable. Eccles gets summarily booed off at the end of the play and is left to a fate of drinking himself to death. The theatre mounting this production was set within a middle-class area of smart housing, and was run by Marie Wilton and her husband Squire Bancroft. (They had also bought a run-down theatre in the West End of London nicknamed the Dust Hole. They renovated this theatre, decorated it with smart and comfortable furnishings, then reopened it as 'The Prince of Wales'.) Here again an audience and a play were well matched.

These actor managers had power through being economically independent; they were the employers of other actors and stagehands, and they used this status to attract audiences of like-minded people.

Eventually such actor managers were rewarded for their successes with knighthoods and honours, just as they are today. What a difference from the actors in Shakespeare's time who were seen as 'masterless men', with no place in society other than as beggars and travellers. Giving an actor a knighthood shows that society has fully accepted them; it has raised them above most of the rest of the people.

Who were the actors?

Plays were often written as 'star vehicles' for particular actors and actresses, as they are today. Audiences came to expect certain performers to take certain roles and were often highly vocal in expressing their disgust when this did not happen. They also expected certain scenes to be played in certain ways; for example, death scenes performed in an acrobatic style.

The leading actor in the play Black-Ey'd Susan became a big star of his day, thereafter specialising in similar roles. This good-looking actor, T.P. Cooke, continued to perform roles that were specially written to allow him to use his considerable physicality and an ability to evoke pathos and sympathy. His performances were noted for fast emotional switching between comedy, sorrow, fights and tears. Audiences became emotionally involved with the actor as well as with their performance, just as they do today in star-vehicle productions. Compare this with contemporary comedies and musicals, where actors play up to their well-known strengths. This practice was clearly rooted in the Victorian Music Hall.

There were, of course, serious actors that emerged during this era. Ellen Terry (1847–1928) was born into a theatrical family and made her first theatrical appearance as a child. Terry played many roles throughout her life and became highly celebrated. She went on to perform a wide range of plays, eventually becoming a member of Henry Irving's Lyceum Theatre Company, where she specialised in major Shakespearean roles.

In 1903, Terry took over her own theatre, the Imperial, which she ran with her son and her business partner, Henry Irving. Here she became the archetypal actor manager, with complete control over what plays she chose to both mount and perform in. She specialised in the works of George Bernard Shaw and Henrik Ibsen; she toured America to huge acclaim and eventually went on to star in films.

Actor managers are less common today. Generally performances are mounted by theatrical impresarios and production houses, and are even spin-offs from contemporary TV programmes.

Theatre styles and acting techniques

Theatre was undergoing an immense period of change during the 19th and early 20th centuries. At the beginning of this period, romanticism was the key form, followed by melodrama, the **well-made play**, **farce**, **realism**, **naturalism** and **expressionism**. This is the period when the true foundations of contemporary theatre developed.

Taking it further

Try to find out when the play you will see was written. Did the playwright have a particular actor in mind for the starring role? Did the performance of an actor set the standard for future performances? Where was it first performed and who might have seen it?

Key terms

well-made play
expressionism
farce
realism

Melodrama

This theatre form employs stock characters that represent good and evil; there are heroes and villains, victims and murderers. A good example is *The Streets of London* by Dion Boucicault (1864) where the setting was much more domestic than earlier melodramas.

The form has further developed in pantomime, and it shares many of the same values. The aim is to amuse, shock and often titillate the audience, without challenging the status quo.

The operettas of Gilbert and Sullivan were extremely popular Victorian melodramatic forms along with, among others, the works of Oscar Wilde.

Realism and naturalism

With developments in the processes of staging plays came changes in the types of plays that were being written. We have already seen how plays and audiences each affect the other. This movement began in France with realism, brought about through an increased interest in science and a desire to write about the human condition, but soon spread throughout Europe.

Naturalism was a conscious development from realism, one that meant that plays would explore the workings of the real world, bringing social issues to light and 'curing' them, almost like a doctor might cure a patient's ills. The work of Konstantin Stanislavski in Moscow transformed the way plays were experienced by introducing the concept of 'the fourth wall', removing **soliloquies**, **asides** and **monologues**, and designing sets that closely represented the world in which the play was set; for example, for performances of Chekhov's plays the props include some live crickets, to ensure the noises of these insects would be authentic.

Stanislavski was an influential theatre practitioner, and his ideas are still used today, albeit in a more diluted form than the actors in his company, the **Moscow Arts Theatre**, would have been exposed to. He saw acting as a system of enquiry, where actors must strive to find the truth of their character through exploration of their own emotional memory. Stanislavski's 'System' transformed the ways actors worked forever, and his ideas formed the basis of actors' training at many institutions across the world, such as The Actors' Studio in New York.

Major playwrights of this era are Henrik Ibsen, August Strindberg, Anton Chekhov and George Bernard Shaw.

Expressionism

This kind of theatre can be seen in some of the plays of August Strindberg. These works deal with spiritual awakenings, like the one Alice experiences in *The Dance of Death.* Expressionist plays often depict the struggles between established authority and the protagonists, and they deal with the expression of emotions. Expressionist plays were not written to realistically depict life and social issues, as did realistic or naturalistic plays, rather they explore the struggles rooted in society. Ibsen and Strindberg are key playwrights of this movement that would further develop well into the 20th century.

These writers' work spans this and the previous major theatre movements, as their plays developed to reflect and influence changes in society.

Key terms

soliloquy
aside
monologue
Moscow Arts Theatre

Taking it further

Think about a play written for the naturalistic period. You can find some suitable plays on page 154 of the AS *Drama Theatre Studies Student Book*. These are all by Anton Chekhov. There is also a section about Stanislavski's system for training actors for the naturalistic theatre. How would you show someone which different elements of the play give information about the space it was written for? For example, are there descriptions of how the set is to be arranged, such as in a room, with furniture and props? Are natural sounds called for in the directions on the text? Do the directions describe the location of the play in detail?

Activity 1

a) How did the production of a play you have seen differ from the way it might have been staged originally?

b) How might the acting style have been different?

c) Try working on a scene from your play as if you were preparing for a naturalistic performance. Use some of Stanislavski's exercises to help you, such as thinking about an experience of your own that is similar to something experienced by your character.

d) Now try playing the scene as if you know the audience is there; make contact with them directly. How does this change the experience for both you and the audience?

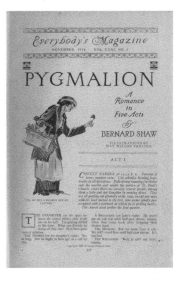

The social, cultural and political context

The physical aspects of a production during this time developed, in part, as a result of the exploration of the stage as a backdrop to the action, and as the environment for the action. This ties in with the growth of knowledge about the world, science and technology.

With developments in the understanding of psychology, there was increasing interest in plays about the human psyche. However, there was also enthusiasm for plays dealing with society, its customs and foibles. The plays of Oscar Wilde deal hilariously with these issues. *The Importance of Being Earnest* and *Lady Windermere's Fan* remain popular today because they are brilliantly written, extremely funny and expose the nature of class and gender divisions in ways that still interest contemporary audiences.

Politically this was a time of massive upheaval, culminating in the start of the First World War. (See the table of historical and theatrical events on page 144.) In many areas of Europe and the United States society was changing, accompanied by wars and violence, and this is reflected in the theatre of the time.

Interpretation

Think about the performance of a play from this era that you have seen recently. Ask yourself some questions to help you determine what sort of director's interpretation you have experienced:

• What was the director trying to communicate through their production?

• What form of theatre was it? Naturalistic, expressionistic or melodramatic?

• What was the acting style used? Were there several?

• Were any cuts or changes made in the scenes or dialogue? Why?

• What technical and design ideas were employed, and how different were they from those used when the play was originally performed?

Working on the text

As you work on the text you have chosen, you will divide your activities between practical work in the studio and research in the library and on the internet. This is how you will get to know the text really well. It is most important that you find out how to bring the play alive, as a piece of performance, because this is what the exam is asking you to write about.

Activity 2

Imagine you are waiting to go on stage to perform a role in your chosen play, in its original theatre, on the first night. Think about the audience – who are they? What are you wearing and what props are you carrying? How do you get to your entrance and what can you see, smell and hear as you make your way to the stage? When you get on stage, what is the audience's first reaction?

Activity 3

Here are some practical activities using the text:

a) Choose a key scene. Play the scene a few times, exploring ways you can deliver the language.

b) Create a modern version of the scene using today's language. Does this help you get to the real meaning of the scene?

c) Working on the scene, try to find out the emotional truth in the writing. Try performing it very naturalistically, as you might do for television; then try using large movements and gestures, much like a pantomime character might play the lines. Does this tell you anything about what the writer is trying to say through these lines?

d) Perform the scene entirely in movement; try to express the emotions of your character as fully as possible; add the lines and explore the differences between your two versions.

e) Take it in turns to direct each other in a scene, exploring different objectives and the relationships between characters.

f) Try to find out about the space or stage used for the original performance of the play. This will help you explore how the original production was staged and how the director used space to create meaning for the audience.

g) Get hold of some pieces of costume, e.g. rehearsal skirts, hats, formal jackets or boots, which correspond to the costume of the period. See how this affects your movement on stage. This exercise can also be applied to props, especially 'costume' props, like fans and swords.

h) Try playing comic scenes with an audience which participates (i.e. other members of your group). Place 'audience' members in positions they might occupy in the original theatre. What effect does this have on how you play the scene?

i) Experiment with scene changes and how scenes are separated by pauses, or how they might run into each other. What is the effect of having one scene follow another very quickly, with the second group of actors coming on while the first group are still making their exit? What is gained or lost by a slower scene change, perhaps accompanied by music?

Preparing for the live production

When you know which play you will be seeing for this part of Unit 4, you can start researching what was happening when it was written and first performed. Use the table of historical events on page 144 to help you put the work in context.

- What was happening when the play was written and performed?

- Where was it first performed?

- Who directed it? (It may be difficult to find this out.)

- What kind of theatre was the piece first performed in, and how did it differ from the one in which you will experience it?

- Bearing in mind that theatres are built, and plays are written, for different types of audience (refer back to *Black-Ey'd Susan*), who do you think might have enjoyed this play?

- Read the play. What are the key themes? Who are the key players? Write down your thoughts and think about which aspects you will look out for during the performance.

Preparing for the theatre visit

This is a key moment in your course and you want to make the most of it. It may be helpful to refer back to pages 67–68 of the AS Student Book for general advice on the evaluation of a live performance. This will remind you of areas to consider.

Before the visit

It's a good idea to reread the text slowly, remembering all the work you've done on it. Check through your notes, flagging up key points for yourself about the original staging. Research the theatre where the performance is taking place. Most theatres will have photographs on their websites, or online booking diagrams showing the shape of the theatre and auditorium. Research the company which is staging the play. Are they well known for any particular style or approach to texts from earlier periods? Look at their marketing and publicity material; does it tell you what their approach will be?

During the performance

When you go into the theatre, compare it with the theatre in which your play was originally staged. Make some initial notes before the play starts about the audience, theatre and acting area. It might be helpful to have a checklist to write quick notes against. Get a programme and read the notes if you have time. If not, read them later.

Further reading

Tom Waits' website has a range of articles, clips and reviews of his production in 2000, including lyrics to some of his songs, composed for the production: http://www.tomwaitslibrary.com/woyzeck-main.html
Waits' CD *Blood Money* (Epitaph/ANTI, 2002) has his songs for the play.

Further reading

Benn, M., *The Drama of Revolt: A Critical Study of Georg Büchner (Anglica Germanica Series 2)*. Cambridge University Press, 1979.

Keith-Smith, B., *Büchner in Britain: A Passport to Georg Büchner*. Mellen Press, 1987.

Leacroft, R., *The Development of the English Playhouse. An Illustrated Survey of Theatre Building in England from Medieval to Modern Times*. Cassell, 1988.

Richards, D.G., *Georg Büchner's Woyzeck: A History of its Criticism*. Boydell and Brewer, 2001.

Russell-Brown, J., *The Oxford Illustrated History of Theatre*. Oxford University Press, 1995..

Styan, J.L., *Modern Drama in Theory and Practice: Realism and Naturalism*. Cambridge University Press, 1981.

Styan, J.L., *The English Stage, a History of Drama and Performance*. Cambridge University Press, 2008.

Wallis, M., and Shepherd, S., *Studying Plays*. Arnold, 1998.

Useful website:

http://www.theatron.org

Give yourself time to make notes at the interval and the end. Reflect on your images of the original production, and note areas of contrast. Try to spot if cuts or alterations have been made to the text. One obvious area of difference will be the use of stage technology. Note how lights, sound, projection and special effects are used, and how effective they are. Do they add significantly to the effect of the performance? If so, how?

Note down all the thoughts you have had. Discuss the play with others, but don't lose your own impressions. Make more notes when you get home, or the following morning. Look again at the programme.

Preparing for the exam

You are not allowed any pre-published material in the exam, only your own notes. These may be up to 1,000 words, but may also include drawings, sketches and diagrams. You should include visual information where relevant, for example sketches of the original playing space and the one you saw used in performance. Your notes should focus on the comparisons and contrasts which you have observed. It is helpful to include key terms (for example, 'proscenium'), ensuring that they are correctly spelt.

In the exam

Read the question, and think about it. You know that it will be focusing on the contrast between *then* and *now*, but what specifically is it asking you? Is the focus on the acting? The direction? The stage technology? The design? Make notes about the relevant areas. Put these in order as your plan of your answer. Write a brief introduction and then the main part of your answer. Read it through, and then write a brief conclusion. Read it through again.

E X A M Z O N E

This section is about you as an informed member of an audience responding to a live production of a play written and originally performed in one of the following three time periods:

- 525BC–AD65
- 1564–1720
- 1828–1914.

You will see and respond to a live production of the chosen play and connect this response back to your understanding of the original performance conditions of the play.

Note that the period chosen for Section C must be different from the one in which the play chosen for Sections A and B was written. If, for example, *Doctor Faustus* is the chosen text for exploration, then Section C must be a performance of any play written and originally performed in either 525BC–AD65 or 1828–1914. Your teacher will be aware of the restrictions for this section, but it is worth considering this carefully when planning an approach to the unit as a whole.

Your experience of live theatre in the AS year will help you with preparing for this section. You will be responding to how a director sets out to engage you with an interpretation of a text, and what elements of theatre are used during that production to assist your understanding as a member of that audience. You will go to the theatre with Unit 4 in mind and you will need to be alert to the production and how it sets out to engage you. You will be there as an informed member of the audience, an active participant in the production, rather than a passive observer. There will be a collective and a personal response to the production and you will have opinions on a range of elements afterwards. Your personal views will be the ones that form the core of your notes that you can take into the exam with you. There is a maximum of 1,000 words allowed, and this should be more than enough for you to compile information to jog your memory during the exam. It is a good idea to start with the live performance notes first and then cut the historical context ones into them, so you have a set of notes that mixes and matches across the two time periods.

It is likely that you will have carried out some research into the original performance conditions of the play before you see it, but this will depend on your own timescale in your school or college. You will need to have notes that reflect the social, cultural and historical elements of the chosen time period, and you will need to consider the live performance in relation to how it might have been produced originally, and what impact it might have had on the audience of the time.

You might look at your notes under the following headings:

Now	Then
• What did I see?	• What might they have seen?
• What did I hear?	• What might they have heard?
• What did I think about it?	• What might they have thought about it?

> **Tip**
>
> You can save yourself words in your research notes by using 'prompts' – words or phrases which trigger your memory, so you don't need to write everything out in detail.

> **Tip**
>
> Remember that the exam question will ask you to discuss comparisons and contrasts between **then** and **now** in relation to the production of your chosen text. Make sure all your notes are relevant.

> **Tip**
>
> Do not write notes during the production. It stops you enjoying the performance and can be very irritating for the performers.

EXAMZONE

These are very basic headings, but they also provide you with a structure for your notes and give you an opportunity to focus on the historical context in relation to the live experience. The notes are intended to be reminders of the experience and to jog your memory in the exam. How you set them out is up to you, but make sure they are accessible in the exam room. The word limit of 1,000 words is approximately two sides of A4 typed at size 12 font. It might be helpful to tape a sheet of notes on the live production to your sheet of notes on the historical context. If your headings across the double page correspond, then you can easily compare aspects of the production now and then. Your two sheets might look something like this:

As You Like It, Royal Shakespeare Theatre, Stratford upon Avon, May 2009 Director: Michael Boyd	Historical period: 1564–1720
Acting	Acting
Design: Set	Design: Set
Costume/make-up	Costume/make-up
Lighting/sound	Lighting/sound
Director's interpretation	Director's interpretation
What I thought of it	What they might have thought of it

There are other ways of setting out your notes, but you need to remember that 1,000 words is not a lot and that the response to the question must connect your experience of the live performance with your understanding of its historical context. The more successful you are at making the connection, the more marks you will gain. These notes are there to support your thinking and to jog your memory – they are not the answer to the question.

EXAMZONE

There is a choice of two questions in Section C, and one of the questions will always start with a quotation. If you are answering this question, it is important that you make reference to the quotation throughout the response, so that your examiner knows that you are taking it into account. Both questions require you to refer to the experience you have had as a member of an audience, and to make the connection back to the original performance conditions of the play that you have seen live. You know you will be required to do this before you go into the exam room, so it is important that you have notes that will help you to make the connections.

Your response to the live production is your response; the examiner may or may not have seen the production you are writing about and may or may not agree with your response, but that is not relevant as long as you present a considered argument. When introducing historical facts into your answer, you need to make sure that it does not read like a history essay. In preparing for this section, you could practise structuring sentences and paragraphs that move across the time periods as a matter of course; for example, you might start a response to a question about the use of special effects in the following way:

> I was engaged from the moment we entered the auditorium with the sounds of the forest echoing through the theatre, quietly at first and getting louder up to the moment when the lights went up on a forest scene at dawn. There was a mist hanging over the stage, created by dry ice, and giving the effect of being in a different world and time. I thought it was effective at creating the mood and atmosphere and, I think some suspense at the start of the performance. This use of effects to engage an audience at the start of a production would not have been possible in its original performance conditions, but the performance would have started with a live fanfare to let the audience know that it was time to gather as the performance was about to begin.

In this example, there is a clear reference to the live experience and a connection made to the original performance conditions at the same point in the production. If you choose key moments during the production, and explore how they might have been presented in the original performance, this will give you opportunities to compare and contrast in relation to the demands of the question.

The candidate in this extract also makes a comment on the effectiveness of the opening of the live performance, and it is this kind of comment that helps to lift a response into the Level 5 band. This is the kind of response you can practise regularly in preparing for Unit 4. In just the same way as you would want a performance to engage your audience in the first couple of minutes, you need to be thinking about how to engage your examiner in the opening paragraph of your response.

The questions in Section C have to be generic as the exam board does not know what you have been to see in relation to which time period, so they need to cover all possibilities. Your answer, however, must be specific and must draw your examiner into your understanding of that live production in relation to its historical context. As a student of drama and theatre studies, it is expected that you will have something to say about the theatre you have seen.

Glossary of drama and theatre terms

Absurd (absurdist): the performance style of Steven Berkoff, the characters will often be quite bizarre and almost unreal; certainly larger than life.

Action: the events that happen in a drama or play and that an audience witnesses taking place on stage.

Actioning: technique which assumes that every spoken sentence is delivered with a specific intention – and that this intention changes with each sentence.

Actions: what a character does in a play. Actions may be physical or psychological, but will usually impact on the plot and on other characters as well as on the individual who initiates the action.

Agon: the main argument, debate or dispute of the plot in a Greek play.

Alienated: where theatre makes something that we normally take as familiar, strange and unfamiliar.

Aside: a dramatic convention in which an actor addresses the audience, while the other characters are unaware that he or she is doing so.

Assistant director: assists the director by taking notes on all moves and other decisions and keeping them together in the prompt copy. This task is often done by the stage manager because there is no assistant.

Audience focus: where the audience's attention is being focused by the performers and/or technical effects.

Auditorium: the part of the theatre in which the audience sits. Also known as the House.

Avenue staging: staging of a performance with the audience placed on two sides, as though the performance space is a street.

Backdrop: a large painted curtain going across the back of the stage, often picturing landscapes, vistas or rooms, depending on the needs of the production, sometimes simply a decorative illustration of angels, cherubs or animals.

Black comedy: dark, sardonic humour that examines the bleakest, most controversial or political of topics.

Blackout: switching all stage lights out at once, leaving the stage in complete darkness. (See also Dead blackout.)

Blank verse: unrhymed lines with an underlying rhythm and a standard length.

Blocking: the setting of the actors' positions and moves at the beginning of rehearsals.

Boal: Augusto Boal was an Argentinean theatre practitioner, born in 1931, who invited his audiences to become involved in his theatre performances, asking them to change what they were watching.

Brainstorming: putting down all ideas in a spontaneous manner.

Breeches parts: parts written in Restoration plays specially to allow actresses to display their legs, adding to the sexiness of the play.

Café Concert: this style of entertainment began in Paris and London in the 18th century but came to its height in the 19th century. Performers would perform songs, dances and comedy skits for audiences as they ate and drank; they were often quite bawdy.

Caricature: an exaggerated portrayal of a character usually for comic effect. This can involve emphasising a particular vocal or physical mannerism.

Character: the person/persona that an actor wishes to convey.

Characterisation: the artistic representation of human character or motives.

Choreographer: creates, teaches and rehearses the dance routines.

Choreography: the creative process of putting a series of movements together to create work. Stage fights and dance moves are usually highly choreographed.

Chorus: a group of people working collectively using vocal and movement skills to communicate thoughts, feelings and ideas. In the manner of a classical Greek chorus, they may narrate a story, comment on the action and express an opinion.

Climax: the moment when the threads of the plot or events in the play come together and are satisfactorily resolved. There is a sense in most plays or drama of a build-up in tension towards a climactic point, followed by some kind of resolution.

Cockpit theatre: a roofed theatre with some similarities to an unroofed theatre.

Collage: a 'patchwork' of dialogue, sounds and visual images from different contexts put together to provide an impressionistic presentation.

Comedy: a light-hearted and amusing drama, typically with a happy ending.

Comedy of manners: a comedy that mocks the manners of a particular social class.

Commedia dell'arte (Commedia): an ancient form of travelling improvisational theatre that originated in Italy in the late 16th century.

Conjectural: based upon assumptions drawn from limited evidence.

Conscience corridor (also known as **conscience alley** or **thought tunnel**): a person in a role of which the whole group has prior knowledge, walks through a corridor formed by the group and hears thoughts or questions from each person as they move along. Useful for character building and development.

Convention (theatrical): generally agreed practices and techniques.

Corpsing (corpse): an actor who laughs when they shouldn't is said to 'corpse'. It means they have normally come out of character.

Cross-cutting: changing back and forth between scenes or episodes of action. The first scene runs up to a selected point and the action freezes or the lights fade out on it. Concurrently, the second scene starts and runs up to another 'cutting point'. The action reverts ('cuts') to a section of the first scene. The process of switching between scenes continues.

Cue: the moment when an actor must enter, speak or act; an instruction by the stage manager to one of the technical departments to take some action.

Curtain call: taking a bow in front of the audience at the end of a show; usually abbreviated to 'curtain'.

Dead blackout (DBO): a sudden, instantaneous switching off of all lights.

Designer: usually designs all aspects of the production: set, costumes, wigs, make-up, etc. Sometimes in very large companies these may be separate roles.

Desk: lighting or sound control board.

Devising/devised work: work that is principally developed by performers without working to a script written by a playwright in the conventional sense.

Diction or metre of tragedy: a free-form version of one of the strict Greek regulations of writing more suited to conveying speech.

Director: controls all aspects of the production: develops the concept for the production, briefs the designer and lighting designer, plots the actors' moves, rehearses the actors.

Doubling: the same performer playing more than one role or part in a play; it can also be when more than one player portrays the same role.

Dramatic irony: the situation in which the audience knows more about events on stage than one or more of the characters.

Dramatic tension: a heightened sense of anticipation about what is going to happen next.

End-on staging: the traditional audience seating layout where the audience is looking at the stage from the same direction. This seating layout is that of a Proscenium Arch theatre.

English Renaissance: a cultural and artistic movement dating from the early 16th- to the early 17th-century, linked to the European movement which originated in Italy in the 14th-century: also the Elizabethan era.

Ensemble: performers working together as a group; the members of the cast of a production other than the protagonists or leading players.

Enunciation: clear pronunciation and articulation.

Epic theatre: an early 20th-century theatre form where the purpose of the play is to present ideas to an audience, rather than to provide entertainment; such as in works by Bertolt Brecht.

Everyman character: a character in drama that represents the common man, one for whom things seem to happen that affect his life without his having the power to stop or influence them.

Expressionism (Expressionist): a late 19th- and early 20th-century theatre form that often experimented with making its protagonists suffer so much that their whole life changes as a result.

Fade: to increase (fade up), decrease (fade down) or eliminate (fade out) gradually the brightness of a lantern or the volume of a sound.

Fairy tale: traditional stories often told to children to entertain or scare them, usually with a moral attached.

Farce: a very old theatre form involving highly unlikely plot twists, characters who are disguised or misidentified as someone else, full of sexual jokes and often ending in a wild chase scene.

Flashback: a moment from a character's remembered past. Enacting a flashback can help to gain an understanding of a character's behaviour, emotions and attitude and provide some of the 'back story'.

Footlights: traditionally a series of floodlights placed along the front of the stage on the floor, but rarely used today.

Form: the shape and structure of a drama. It is determined by the content of the drama (e.g. the way the playwright has presented the narrative) and by the way it is presented (the choices made by actors, designers and directors in interpreting the material for performance). Form is often confused with genre, with which it is closely associated. Something classified as naturalistic in terms of genre will be recognised as such by the form it takes.

Forum theatre: a way of working developed by Brazilian director Augusto Boal. Participants sit or stand in a large circle to observe an improvisation. At any point in the proceedings, the performers or observers can stop the action and ask for help or give advice about what to do or say next. The improvisation may continue from the point of interruption or start again, and an observer may decide to take over from one of the performers or join in by taking on another role.

Fourth wall: the notion that the stage is like a room with four walls, with the audience looking in where one of the walls would be. Associated with naturalism in which there is a convention that the performers act as though the audience is not there.

Freeze-frame: during an improvisation or the playing of a scene, the instruction 'freeze' is called out and the performers hold their positions at that moment. It is often confused with 'still image' or 'tableau', which are techniques used to set up a deliberate 'stage picture' or 'frozen image'.

Gallery: 1) the levels of seating areas to the sides of a theatre; 2) the raised level behind the stage of an Elizabethan theatre where musicians could accompany the performance.

Genre: a category or type of drama which is defined by a particular set of conventions and norms. Genres such as comedy, tragedy, musicals, melodrama and pantomime have readily identifiable features, whereas terms such as naturalism, expressionism and epic are more elusive. Difficulties arise because a genre (e.g. naturalism) can be defined by its form (e.g. naturalistic) which can be recognised by certain aesthetic elements (i.e. it has a naturalistic style).

Gesture: a movement of part of the body, especially a hand or the head, to express an idea or meaning.

Gestus: a term associated with the use of gesture. Brecht used it to refer to the attitude or stance of a character in relation to another communicated through behaviour, movement, expressions and intonation. A character's relationship to another is determined by social conditions and conventions. In other words, if two characters are separated by being rich and poor this will predetermine the attitude of one to the other which will come across through gesture irrespective of what is being said.

Given circumstances: in Stanislavskian theory, all of the available information that an actor uses in creating a role.

Greek tragedy: theatre written and performed in ancient Greece where the downfall of a society or its individuals was the subject matter of the work.

Groundling: a member of an Elizabethan audience who stood in the area around the stage (the yard) rather than purchasing seated tickets.

Horseshoe staging: the audience are seated in a horseshoe shape around the stage area.

Hot-seating: a technique used to gain a deeper understanding of a character or role. The group asks an individual relevant questions about their feelings, thoughts, actions or circumstances. The individual answers the questions in role or as they think the character would answer.

Improvisation: performing quickly in response to something, or acting without previous planning. A distinction is made between spontaneous improvisation and prepared improvisation, the former relating to making up a role as you go along and the latter relating to working within a previously agreed structure of ideas and roles.

157

In-the-round staging: a performance space in which the audience surrounds the acting space on all sides.

Kabuki theatre: the highly stylised classical Japanese dance-drama, known for the stylisation of its drama and the elaborate make-up worn by some of its performers.

Komos: the celebratory and uplifting ending of a Greek play.

Lantern: theatrical term for a light. 'Luminaire' is more common nowadays.

LFX: abbreviation for lighting effects in the theatre.

Libretto: the text used in an extended musical work such as an opera or musical.

Lighting designer: responsible for designing, rigging, focusing and plotting the lighting for a production. Works in close cooperation with the designer.

Lyre: a stringed instrument similar to a harp used by the ancient Greeks.

Marking the moment: a convention used to highlight a significant point in a drama. It can be achieved through the use of techniques such as freeze-frame, spotlighting, narrated announcements, projected captions, sound effects, musical underscoring, or change of lighting state.

Melodrama: play where the characters are straightforward and easy to understand, such as villains who will do harm and heroines who need to be saved; the characters drive the action; very popular during the late 19th century and early 20th century.

Metre: the pattern and structure of verse or poetry.

Mime: to act a part using gestures and actions rather than words.

Modernism: a cultural movement that took place in the 19th century where writers and artists explored the human condition and what might be holding society back. They wanted to replace the norms of society with more progressive ideas.

Monologue: literally, one person speaking. It can be a genre in its own right (for example, *Shirley Valentine*), but it can also be a speech by one character in other genres.

Montage: a term taken from film theory, referring to the way a dramatic sequence can be made up of a series of connected but different images edited together. It is rather like collage.

Morality plays: a form of drama popular in the 15th and 16th centuries, where characters personify moral qualities such as pride.

Moscow Arts Theatre, The: the theatre company set up by Constantin Stanislavski and Vladimir Namirovich-Danchenko in Moscow in 1898, through which they explored the mounting of productions in a naturalistic style.

Music Hall: popular in the 19th and early 20th centuries; variety entertainment that presented song and dance, including ballet, comedy sketches, novelty acts such as juggling and magic.

Narration: dialogue designed to tell the story or provide accompanying information. Narration can accompany on-stage action or be presented in its own right.

Narrator: a role that functions like a storyteller. A narrator can be used to describe the action, provide a commentary or give additional information. A narrator can be present on stage or be an off-stage or pre-recorded voice.

Naturalism: a late 19th- and 20th-century style where plays and performers were engaged with presenting the world as it really is, where performers aimed at presenting a genuine and authentic view of the world and society.

Objective: an intention or aim; what a character wants to achieve.

Opéra comique: a French genre of opera that contains spoken dialogue. It emerged out of the popular '*opéra comiques en vaudevilles*' of the Fair Theatres of St Germain and St Laurent.

Pace: the speed at which a scene, action or the whole play takes place.

Parabasis (pl. parabases): where the chorus addresses the audience in a Greek play. (In most of Aristophanes' other comedies, the chorus puts across the playwright's views and often gives advice.)

Parados: the entrance of the Chorus in a Greek play.

Pastiche: a light-hearted imitation of another style.

Personification: representing an abstract quality or idea as a person or creature.

Physical theatre: a 20th-century form where actors use the body to physically represent places, people and action, without the need for many props, set or scenery, such as that practised by Steven Berkoff, Complicite or Pina Bausch.

Pit: the sunken area in front of the stage in which the orchestra sits.

Plot: the sequence of events in a play.

Production: what design and technical elements achieve.

Prologue: the first part of the action before the appearance of the Chorus in a Greek play.

Promenade staging: a form of staging in which the audience moves around to different areas or stages in a performance space. Medieval mystery plays performed on carts and wagons are early examples of this.

Prompt copy (also **Book**): the copy of the script in which all notes, moves and cues are noted.

Proscenium: the permanent or semi-permanent wall dividing the audience from the stage. The opening in this wall frames the stage, hence the **proscenium arch**, the actual opening of a proscenium stage.

Proxemics: used to describe the way in which spatial relationships between each of the performers and between the performers and their stage environment work.

Raked: many stage floors, usually older style, are higher at the back than at the front, to give the audience a better view. The 'rake' is the angle of slope from back to front. In most modern theatres it is the audience seating that is raked, not the stage.

Realism: a genre that sets out to portray everyday life as faithfully as possible. It has its origins in the visual arts during the early part of the 19th century.

Renaissance: European movement of the 14th to 17th centuries marked by a surge of intellectual activity and a revival of classical learning.

Representational: in a Brechtian manner.

Revolve: a stage, or part of a stage, which can revolve through 360 degrees.

Rhymed verse: where the words at the ends of lines have similar vowel sounds.

Rhythm: the pattern of sounds and movements in a speech or scene.

Role: any part portrayed by an actor in a play. It is used less specifically than 'character' to refer to more representational figures in a drama such as Devil or non-human representations such as War.

Role-play: the act of pretending to be someone (or something) else. Role-play is generally confined to taking on a clearly defined role such as a doctor without any attempt at in-depth psychological analysis or understanding.

Role reversal: an exercise performed during an improvisation or rehearsal for a scene, in which the actors reverse the roles/characters they are portraying in order to gain a different view or understanding of their own role.

Rostrum: a moveable platform often used to provide levels on stage.

Satire: a literary work which holds up human vices and follies to ridicule.

Satirical comedy: often edgy and insightful.

Satyr play: comic play of ancient Greece with a mythological theme and chorus representing satyrs.

Set: the scenery for a particular show or individual scene.

SFX: abbreviation for sound effects in the theatre.

Sightlines: the lines of sight from the extremities of the seating area in the auditorium to the stage; sightlines allow a designer to calculate how much of the set can be seen.

Slapstick comedy: a form of physical comedy where the performers use tumbling and often apparent clumsiness to raise a laugh from their audiences, such as in the silent films of Buster Keaton.

Soliloquy: a speech delivered by a character to themselves rather than to another character, thereby revealing their thoughts to the audience.

Soundscape: an aural environment created for a scene using sounds made vocally. Each individual creates a sound appropriate for a given circumstance to accompany or introduce a scene. Repeated words and phrases overlapping each other can also be used to suggest a location or might be portrayed as sounds in a character's head, as though from a nightmare or series of flashbacks.

Space-staging: where the action happens amongst the audience.

Spontaneous improvisation: see improvisation.

Spotlighting: a technique in which an improvisation or playing of a scene is replayed, but the action is redefined by focusing attention on a selected area of the performance space. This can be done with the use of lighting or by marking the floor area so that any action that previously happened outside these confines no longer takes place.

Stage manager (SM): in charge of everything that happens backstage and all other backstage crew. The SM also attends most rehearsals and often compiles 'the Book'. Once a show starts its run, they take complete control for running the show.

Staging: putting on a play; bringing a piece to the stage.

Stereotype: a conventional and oversimplified concept, opinion or image; a person who is regarded as embodying or conforming to a set image or type.

Still image: creating a picture to represent a frozen moment or to sum up what is happening in a drama. It is a useful technique to explore the effects of positioning characters in relation to one another in terms of levels and proximity and to demonstrate non-verbal communication.

Storyboard: a series of images and/or text showing the sequence of the action planned for a play.

Stürm und Drang: ('Storm and Stress') movement that had been prevalent in Germany in the late 18th century. This was a movement of young male writers who were concerned with the trials and tribulations of the ordinary, common man.

Style: the aesthetic quality of a drama. Often indistinguishable from genre and form, style refers to the way the actors are performing, the visual characteristics of the setting and costumes, and the choice of particular conventions. A drama belonging to one genre (such as naturalism) can be presented in different styles (for example, the acting may be in a naturalistic style but the stage design can be in an abstract style).

Sub-plot: lesser plot beneath the main plot of a drama.

Sub-text: in narrative terms, a secondary plot or storyline. In terms of acting and character analysis, it refers to the idea that there are other meanings below the surface of what is actually being said and done.

Tableau(x): a variation on still image, referring to a dramatic grouping of characters. A tableau may not necessarily be a still or frozen image, as dialogue can be spoken and gestures used when it refers to the general stage picture during a sequence in a scene.

Techniques: drama forms, exercises, strategies and conventions that are widely used to develop understanding and explore meaning through the drama process.

Tempo: speed.

Theme: a recurring idea or set of ideas in a play.

Thespian: an actor.

Thought-tracking: an exercise that allows the inner thoughts of a character or role to be heard out loud. It is often used in conjunction with freeze-frame or still image where a participant is asked to say what they are thinking at that point in time.

Thrust staging: a type of stage which projects out into the auditorium and has audience seated on three sides.

Tone: the quality of the voice when speaking, indicating the attitude of the speaker.

Tragedy: a form of theatre where the protagonists appear to be drawn down a path of destruction and downfall, where they have no control over what happens to them and they cannot prevent their fate.

Traverse staging: a performance space that has the audience on either side of the stage.

Truck: a rostrum or platform on wheels, on which scenery can be mounted so that it can be rolled into any position on stage.

Vision: the director's interpretation or picture of what he wishes to achieve.

Vista stage: an additional area upstage of the main acting area which could be revealed to show set elements (backcloths, flats, etc.) to provide a visual background for scenes set on the main stage. Not used as an acting area, it added to the depth of the stage picture.

Well-made play: a form of 19th-century theatre begun in France, where plays presented action, much of which had already happened before the play had begun. There would be many plot complications and sub-plots, twists and false endings, often involving characters who were not who they seemed to be.

Published by:

 u18633

THOMAS TALLIS SCHOOL LIBRARY

Pearson Education Limited, a company incorporated in England and Wales, having its registered office at Edinburgh Gate, Harlow, Essex, CM20 2JE.

Registered company number: 872828

Edexcel is a registered trademark of Edexcel Limited

Text © Carolyn Carnaghan, John Davey, Alan Evans and Steve Lewis 2009

First published 2009

12 11 10 09

10 9 8 7 6 5 4 3 2 1

British Library Cataloguing in Publication Data

A catalogue record for this book is available from the British Library

ISBN 978 1 846902 38 3

Designed and illustrated by: Juice Creative Limited

Original illustrations © Pearson Education Ltd

Printed in Great Britain by Henry Ling Ltd., at the Dorset Press, Dorchester, Dorset

Author team:

Carolyn Carnaghan is a principal examiner for drama, independent arts consultant and writer. John Davey is Head of School, Performing Arts, Kingston College, Surrey. Steve Lewis is Director for Visual and Performing Arts, City College Brighton and Hove. Alan Evans and Ginny Spooner are senior examiners.

The publishers are grateful to Alan Perks, senior examiner, for his consultancy and contribution.

Credits:

The publisher would like to thank the following individuals and organisations for permission to reproduce copyright material:

Nicholas Gibbs from the interview with Max Stafford-Clark, 2002 http://www.masktheatre.co.uk/frommemb/maxstaf.htm, copyright © 2002 Nick Gibbs; Independent News and Media Limited for an extract from "Malicious, misguided, and badly misinformed" *The Independent on Sunday* 2 April 2008 copyright © Independent News and Media Limited 2008; Solo Syndication for an extract from "Immigration timebomb: Lies that created a soaring population" *The Daily Mail* 22 October 2007 copyright © Solo Syndication 2007; and W.W. Norton & Company, Inc for an extract from "The Elements of Drama" by Carl E. Bain from *The Norton Introduction to Literature*, Combined Shorter Edition edited by Carl E. Bain, Jerome Beaty & J. Paul Hunter. Copyright © 1973 by W. W. Norton & Company, Inc. Used by permission of W.W. Norton & Company, Inc.

Alamy Images: Peter Barritt 128; INTERFOTO Pressebildagentur 105; Peter Oshkai 125; **Arenapal:** Henrietta Butler 80; Marilyn Kingwill 96; **Brown University Library:** Shaw Collection 149; **Corbis:** Bettmann 84; **DK Images:** De Agostini Editore Picture Library 77; **Getty Images:** Matt Cardy 33; Nobby Clark 129; Andrea Pistolesi 137; **Robbie Jack Photography:** 111; **Photolibrary.com:** Digital Vision 26; **Rex Features:** Alastair Muir 14, 17

With thanks to Mill Hill School, London, for Case Studies 3-4.

All other images © Pearson Education

Every effort has been made to contact copyright holders of material reproduced in this book. Any omissions will be rectified in subsequent printings if notice is given to the publishers.

Disclaimer

This Edexcel publication offers high-quality support for the delivery of Edexcel qualifications.

Edexcel endorsement does not mean that this material is essential to achieve any Edexcel qualification, nor does it mean that this is the only suitable material available to support any Edexcel qualification. No endorsed material will be used verbatim in setting any Edexcel examination/assessment and any resource lists produced by Edexcel shall include this and other appropriate texts.

Copies of official specifications for all Edexcel qualifications may be found on the Edexcel website - www.edexcel.com

Websites

The websites used in this book were correct and up to date at the time of publication. It is essential for tutors to preview each website before using it in class so as to ensure that the URL is still accurate, relevant and appropriate. We suggest that tutors bookmark useful websites and consider enabling students to access them through the school/college intranet.